Morel Hunting

JOHN AND THERESA MAYBRIER

STACKPOLE
BOOKS

0 11557 00834 0

Do you want more mushrooms? Do you?
For our dear friend, Larry Lonik, "The Mushroom Man"

Copyright © 2004, 2010 by John and Theresa Maybrier

Published by
STACKPOLE BOOKS
5067 Ritter Road
Mechanicsburg, PA 17055
www.stackpolebooks.com

Printed in the United States of America

Chapter 7 was published in modified form in *Adventure Sports Outdoors* magazine in August 2004.

10 9 8 7 6 5 4

Library of Congress Cataloging-in-Publication Data

Maybrier, John.
    Morel hunting / John and Theresa Maybrier.
        p. cm.
    Includes index.
    ISBN-13: 978-0-8117-0834-0 (pbk.)
    ISBN-10: 0-8117-0834-9 (pbk.)
    1. Morels. 2. Cooking (Morels) I. Maybrier, Theresa. II. Title.
QK623.M65M39 2010
641.3'58—dc22
                                    2010040715

Contents

Introduction

Few things are as exciting and enjoyable as mushroom hunting. We have introduced hundreds of people to mushroom hunting, and to date, no one has said it wasn't the sport for them. We have heard squeaks and squeals, yips and hollers. The joy of the hunt is the enjoyment of the woods in the springtime, the thrill of finding the elusive morel, and the pure pleasure of eating the bounty of the hunt.

There is an old saying: give a man a fish, feed him a dinner; teach a man to fish and he can feed himself for life. We feel the same way about teaching someone to hunt for morels. Once you get a bug for foraging you'll likely expand into foraging for other types of mushrooms and who knows, maybe wild berries, nuts, and wild herbs.

The morel mushroom is the safest, most recognizable mushroom in the woods. This book is designed to introduce you to the joy of foraging for morels, how to find and identify them, and then what to do with them once you find them.

Our experience as guides on group mushroom hunts, along with our personal experience as "chasers" (people who follow mushrooms north as the season moves north) and commercial pickers, and our travels on the sport show circuit have given us the background to do seminars, teach classes, and write this book. In this book we want to share what we know about the growing habits of morels and how to hunt them so that everyone can be better at the sport of mushroom hunting, as well as preserving and preparing mushrooms.

PART I

The Sport of Morel Hunting

The sport of morel hunting is a springtime ritual for more than fifteen million mushroom hunters. That's more than deer and turkey hunters combined. Yet there is very little marketing to the mushroom hunter, little knowledge of the rules and regulations for hunting public grounds; nor are there many books like this one educating people about how to hunt, preserve, and prepare mushrooms properly. The lack of knowledge has built up the mystique of mushroom hunting, partly because many people are afraid of mushroom poisoning (fungophobia), and partly because mushroom hunters don't want to share their experiences because the season is short. Fifty years ago morel mushrooms were abundant.

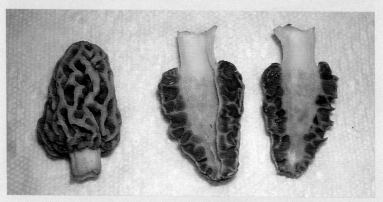

A morel outside and inside.

However, the population of morels is down substantially, and current hunters want all the mushrooms for themselves.

Morels are the safest mushroom to hunt. They are the only springtime mushrooms in the woods that look like sea sponges (thus called sponge mushrooms) and have hollow stems that become the cap. Not only are morels the easiest to identify, but they also are the safest to pick and eat. For over fifty years morels have been harvested in the wild for worldwide distribution. There have been no recorded deaths associated with the morel mushroom.

This book will help anyone learn how to find, identify, and collect morels. We'll not only teach you where and how to find morels and identify them, but also how to preserve them to eat year round and how to prepare them properly.

All fungus has bacteria in it, making it hard to digest. Wild mushrooms should always be cooked properly so that they are more digestible. Basic cooking methods and some great recipes are in chapters 11 and 12.

Keep in mind, the first time you try any new variety of mushroom, try a small amount. If you have no adverse reaction within twenty four hours, enjoy!

All in a day's work!

CHAPTER 1

Identifying Morels

There are five basic varieties of morels. All five varieties of this springtime treat share three simple characteristics. First, it looks like a sea sponge; second, it is hollow; and third, if you cut the morel in half from top to bottom, the cut line (outline) of the morel is continuous. If not, it is not a morel. The half-cap morel has the same outline, but part of the cap extends beyond the point where the cap and stem meet. The false morel or *Verpa* mushroom, which resembles the true half-cap morel, has a cotton-like substance inside the stem stock, and the cap joins the stem up inside the cap with a very definable junction. The cap can be easily knocked off, and the two parts seem very distinct.

Morels show up in the spring in the following order: The first variety is *Morchella antigusticeps*, commonly referred to as the black morel, which appears when daytime temperatures are in the high fifties to low sixties for four or five days after a full week without a freeze. Then *Morchella semilibera*, commonly known as half-cap or half-free, shows up when daytime temperatures rise to the low to mid sixties. *Morchella deliciosa*, the gray morel, appears when daytime temperatures reach the high sixties. *Morchella esculenta*, the yellow morel, appears when daytime highs reach the low seventies, and finally the big foot or *Morchella crassipes* appears when the daily high temperatures reach the high seventies. The season ends when the daytime temperatures are in the eighties for a few days. The last three varieties are referred to as the whites. Each of the varieties has a short window of growth relating to its temperature zone. Our experience is that everyone has their favorite variety to hunt and eat.

VARIETIES OF MORELS

We used to think our friend Larry Lonik liked the black morels best because he was from Michigan where black morels are more abundant, but he really liked them so much because their flavor is deeper and meatier, and they are more aromatic than the other varieties. Besides flavor, our favorite thing about the black morels is that they grow in patches and they signify the beginning of the morel mushroom season. When you find a black morel take time to

Black morels so thick we're picking on our hands and knees.

look around. This variety is usually out in the open at the onset of the season. Usually the only groundcover is leaves; black morels should be easy to see. However, like the other varieties they sometimes can be harder to see. Often, the shadows of leaves look like black morels. When the black morels are taller later in the season (which can be as short as a week depending on how quickly the temperatures rise) they stand up like little witch's caps on the ground. As the season progresses, the black morels can be found in the open, near trees and under or near the shade of evergreen trees if it gets too warm for them. Look for any woodsy area

The odd-looking morel, the half-cap morel, looks like a sea sponge on the outside and is hollow on the inside. Part of the cap hangs over the stem.

with good leaf litter. Look up for areas of blue sky between the canopy of the trees where the sun can pour in and warm the ground. You'll likely find the first black morels in these areas. Once you spot one, mark it with something bright (like a Team Morel Sporebag in safety orange). Take time to look in all directions. Black morels usually grow in groups, and once you spot one morel you can often find others in the same patch. By repeating the same pattern throughout the woods, you will find a lot of black morels. Following the pattern is discussed more thoroughly in chapter 7.

The half-cap morels have very long stems with much smaller caps resembling those of black morels. They have less body and texture. The moisture content is higher and the half-cap morel falls apart in the cooking process. This is the odd-looking morel. Think of it like the Granny Smith apple, which is green when apples are usually red. Part of the cap of the half-cap morel hangs over the stem, unlike other morel varieties. We refer to the half-cap morel as the cooking morel; used as a flavoring for roasted meats and soups, they are incredible. The half-caps are sweeter with a somewhat fruity flavor. These are fun mushrooms to hunt because, like the black morels, they grow out in the open, with little groundcover, and grow in patches. One spring in southern Illinois we picked hundreds of these little treasures. We had so many, and because of their high moisture content we knew they would not dry. With some quick thinking on John's part, we went to the big K and purchased the largest electric skillet they had, along with butter, bacon, and baggies. On the balcony of our hotel we rendered down six skillets full of half-cap mushrooms and three pounds of bacon. We used nearly every baggie in the box. We froze them, and through the winter John cooked them on everything from wild rabbit to a standing rib roast for Thanksgiving dinner. It doesn't get much better than that. The recipe and storage method are described on page 100.

Interestingly though, many people are afraid of the half-cap morel. Some think it is poisonous, others simply don't understand it. In Michigan where a lot of people pick Verpa mushrooms (which can be harmful) they won't pick half-cap morels. In

Morels are the first responders to feed on the decay of a dying tree.

Nebraska many people think these are poisonous. At the sport show in Omaha we spend much of our time debunking this myth. Enjoy these mushrooms. Because so many hunters leave the half-cap behind, there are a lot of them out there.

The white morel family includes the little gray, white, and giant (yellow) varieties. These are the *esculenta* and *deliciosa* and *crassipes* morels. In the Midwest—Missouri, Iowa, Nebraska, Illinois, Indiana, and Ohio—these are the favored morels. In these states a lot of folks don't even know about black and half-cap morels, and those who do often think black morels are spoiled or frozen and half-caps are poisonous.

The white morel varieties have much thicker cap walls, with deeply pitted grooves, and taste like steak. They can be the most frustrating morels to locate. Frequently we have found a single standing gray or yellow mushroom. As much as we know about the habits of morels, we still find these to be some of the most frustrating mushrooms to find. Perhaps it is because the wind can carry the spore for such a long way that one morel can stand alone in the woods. The white varieties of morels are easier to find by the tree-hunting method, discussed in chapter 8. Look for these varieties under trees that show signs of stress or dying. By this part of the season the buds or perhaps even leaves are on the trees. Trees without buds or leaves are under stress or dying and are therefore good candidates to have the gray and yellow morels growing nearby.

Crassipes, the big foot.

The single most important concept that will help you locate morels is this: Morels are the first responders to feed on the decay of the root material of a dying tree.

The last white morel variety, the big foot or giant morel, marks the end of the season. These are not grown up grays and yellows but a variety with a stem stalk that is much wider at the base, that develops to be soda-can size or larger, and that has a thinner cap wall and a beefsteak-like flavor. Due to their greater size and thinner walls, they are best cut into ringlets and batter fried like onion rings or tempura. Whatever the batter, the texture is enhanced. By the time the *crassipes* morels are in the woods, the grass is up and often tall. We look for these in the low areas near a water source like a pond, creek, or runoff. Because they are the late-season morels and spore when the grasses are up, look for them in the grass, under the deep shade of the trees, and in the cooler places in the woods. They too are a challenge to find, but if you have a competitive nature and want bragging rights for the biggest of the

Gray and yellow mountain morels.

season, this is the one to set your sights on. In areas where the grass isn't so tall these morels can be spotted from a good distance. Their golden color stands out against the green of late spring. It doesn't take a lot of these to fill a mesh collection bag.

There are other varieties of morels (*Morchella hybrida, elata, bispora,* and *conica* to name a few), but in this book we're going to discuss only the common varieties found in most states in the continental United States. Morels are found all around the world where there is a noticeable change of seasons or frost line. Morels do not grow in tropical regions except in high elevations where there is a frost line.

In North America morels move north about one hundred miles per week starting in Mexico in about February and ending in Canada in August or September, depending on the weather (temperatures).

CHAPTER 2

Identification, Growth, and Reproduction

The morel mushroom we eat is the reproductive or fruiting part of an underground organism, much like an apple is to the apple tree. Because of the organisms' adaptability, need for survival, and the fact that it grows underground there is still uncertainty about its exact growth habits. Experts debate how the underground organism functions in relation to specific trees, how the mushroom we eat grows and develops, why some years are good and other years are not. What is certain is that when spring arrives and the temperatures are right, morels begin to grow. In the laboratory morels take two weeks to grow. Long before we see morels in the woods, they are growing deep beneath the leaves. They expand as they grow, like blowing up a balloon they gain height, width, and girth. Growth can be slow, but when the nighttime temperatures rise and rain comes, morels can quadruple in size overnight. Morels grow best in cool, overcast, or shaded conditions. The sun, heat, wind, and dry conditions are the enemy.

One way to determine the age of the morel is to examine its stem. All varieties of morels start out with white to creamy-colored stems, and as they age, the stems darken to a golden color.

In southern Iowa one spring, we scouted the woods for dying trees. Temperatures that spring had been very cool, and we were early for the area. We came across a sixty-foot dying tree with thirty tiny morels tucked into the leaf litter. We didn't want to trample the morels as they grew, so we made our early observation and then backed out so as not to disturb them. Two days later we brought a group of morel hunters in. The morels were slightly larger, and we counted a total of 142 mushrooms. If we had the time to let them grow this would have been an amazing find both in pounds and numbers. Since we weren't going to be around to see that happen, we picked and ate them then instead.

Morel reproduction is complicated because it is hard to observe, but a hunter need only understand that the morel is the fruiting body of an underground organism much like the apple is to the apple tree. Inside the apple are seeds to grow new trees. Spores, which are like seeds, are in the grooves of the morel. Air flows in and circulates through the grooves, pulling the spores out. You cannot shake them loose, but you can help with reproduction by carrying the morels you collect in a mesh bag to allow air to flow through the morel, helping the spores become airborne.

Morels come out of the ground clean. Cutting morels when you collect them keeps dirt out of your bag and out of the grooves of the morels. Dirt can clog the grooves and block spores from releasing. Morels release the most spores when they are drying out. Black mesh collection bags draw the sun's heat, drying the morels

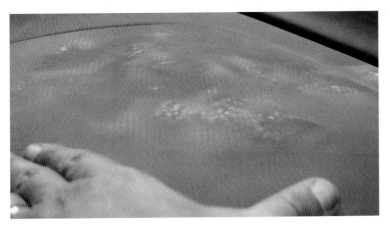

Spore accumulated on our dashboard.

out for quicker distribution of spores. Morels will continue to release spore in your car or refrigerator as long as they are kept cool and dry or until they are fully dried out or immersed in water. More about this later in the section on preserving morels.

You can dry morels on cloudy and cold days; it just takes longer. You can even dry morels in the refrigerator—just put them in a bowl lined with a paper towel, and the spores will collect on the sides of the bowl and paper towel. Morels dry out in dry conditions with or without heat. As soon as the morel begins to surface dry, it begins to release spores for reproduction; as it does this the morel may continue to expand in height and girth if it is protected from direct sunlight, but the deterioration process has

begun. The walls of the morel thin as the spore is expelled from the grooves. The morel is thought to have between 250,000 to 500,000 spores in each cap. Mother Nature has equipped the morel with plenty of "seeds" to ensure its place in the environment.

A morel's growth has much to do with the arrival of spring, along with temperature and moisture. Morels show up when the temperatures reach the high fifties to low sixties after a full week of no frost in places with sufficient moisture. When you find small morels, cover them with leaves and allow them to continue to grow. Leave a few in the sun to see the difference.

Notice the coats. We're drying morels when daytime temperatures are 45 degrees.

When we are traveling and hunting morels, we usually cannot go back the next day to an area where we spotted a morel, but morels grow so slowly that waiting one day will not make much of a difference. We have experimented by placing a mason jar over the body of a morel and checking it the next day. The growth was insignificant. Also, in the midsection of the country, the weather conditions and the bug population can destroy the quality of morels so rapidly that leaving them even a couple of days can be harmful.

The northern states have longer lasting spring seasons with cooler weather longer. There, you can leave morels growing in the shade or in cloudy conditions for several days. The mushrooms can triple in size in four or more days in those conditions. If you live in the northern states and can leave the morels to grow, you will pick more pounds. In the northern states bugs are not as much of a problem either during the cooler spring conditions.

Jason Edge, author of *Find the Tree—Find the Morel*, uses this analogy to describe the growing season for morels in the northern states: "I always compare morels to seed in the garden. A seed planted in early spring takes a lot longer to come up compared to a seed planted in the middle of summer."

A perfect example of this analogy played out in the spring of 2003, when we were guiding hunts in Michigan. The first weekend we picked hundreds of two-inch tall morels in an open area alongside a golf course. Two weeks later we picked hundreds of six- to eight-inch-tall morels in a forest a few miles away. These morels were growing in very different conditions. We were not picking larger mushrooms that were missed before and had grown larger in the meantime. The stems were nearly white; these morels were very fresh. We were picking the same variety of black morel, but it was cool and dry the first weekend and the morels were growing in the sunny open areas of the south-facing slopes. By the third weekend the temperatures had risen and there was plenty of moisture, but the morels were hiding in the shade of the pine trees. Every batch of morels released spore, both the small and the large morels, as we found out by the remains on our dashboard (where we transported them in their mesh bags). Large or small, morels collected in mesh bags leave lots of spore behind for future batches of mushrooms to develop.

Morels are more than ninety percent water. The amount of moisture in the ground has a great deal to do with the size of the morels. Morels, like most mushrooms, need rain to kick-start their growth. If the water table is high from winter thaw or late winter rains, morels will grow to be big enough to be seen easily. Very dry seasons will inhibit size and possibly even deter growth altogether. During drought years be prepared to hunt in low areas near rivers and streams or to travel to more favorable areas.

Traumas such as flooding, fires, and bulldozing cause above-ground vegetation to die, leaving tree and woody bush roots to decay below the ground. Additionally, during such traumas the underground part of the morel senses its demise, and the following spring, the organism will shoot up an extraordinary number of morels (the reproductive part) to insure its survival. Professional pickers follow the burns from the previous year to find and pick enough morels for commercial distribution. Some three to five million pounds of fresh morels are harvested annually and sold worldwide in this way.

Lots of morels after a forest fire.

When a tree or part of a tree dies in the forest, whether from flooding, lightning strikes, or bulldozing, a large number of mushrooms will grow under it. For every bit of tree material above ground there is a mirror-like image of root mass underground that dies too. Fungi feed off the decaying root matter, and when the underground organism has enough energy, it shoots up a morel for reproduction. You don't have to understand all the science to become good at finding mushrooms; you simply have to understand the habits of the mushrooms.

TRUE MORELS

Black morel *(Morchella angusticeps)*

1"–8" tall.

- Season begins when there has been no frost for a week and the daily high temperatures remain in the high 50s to low 60s for 4 or 5 days.
- Has a creamy hollow stem.
- Tan (almost nude) caps on the freshest black morels.
- Ridges darken to black with sun exposure.
- Elongated caps, often shaped like witches' hats, with elongated and grooved pits.

Half-cap morel *(Morchella semilibera)*

3"–8" tall.

- Appears when daily highs are in the mid 60s.
- White to cream, tall, hollow stem, attached midway inside the cap.
- Tan to black-ridged cap similar to that of the black morel but much smaller.

White morels

Gray morel and yellow morel
(Morchella deliciosa and esculenta)

1/2"–8" tall.
- Appears when daily highs rise to the high sixties (gray morels) and then into the seventies (yellow morels).
- White to creamy hollow stems.
- Caps vary from gray to yellow.
- Colors vary like camouflage, blending with the groundcover.
- Thick, deeply pitted walls with wrinkled grooves.

Big foot morel *(Morchella crassipes)*

4"–14+" tall.
- Appears when daily are in the high 70s to low 80s.
- Cream to tan hollow wrinkly stems, broad at the base.
- Thin to thick walls with elongated grooves and shallow pits.

FALSE MORELS

False morels are mushrooms from the same biological family as morels but different species. Think of it like this: we are from the animal kingdom, we are mammals, and we are humans. In the fungi kingdom there is *Morchella* and within *Morchella* are Morel, *Verpa*, and *Gyromitra* mushrooms. False morels are not morels but they are in the *Verpa* and *Gyromitra* families.

False morels fall into two categories: those that are edible and those better left alone. The edibles look more similar to true morels, especially resembling the half-cap morel, but are actually in the *Verpa* family.

Cap or wrinkled mushroom *(Verpa bohemica)*

2"–8" tall.

- Tan-colored caps.
- Cream-colored stems, cottony inside (*not* hollow).
- The wrinkled cap hangs over the top of the stem like a skirt and separates from the stem when picked off.

Thimble or smooth-cap mushroom *(Verpa conica)*

2"–8" tall.

- Tan caps.
- Cream-colored stems, cottony inside (*not* hollow).
- A smooth skirt like cap hangs over the stem and separates from the stem when picked off.

Both of these varieties are edible with caution. They can have a muscle-relaxant effect, particularly if eaten in large quantity with or without morels or when consumed with alcohol. They can even make you go into a coma.

The caps have a meaty flavor but the stems are bitter. Their moisture content is high, and they are difficult to preserve. Collect *Verpa* mushrooms in a separate mesh collection bag because their high moisture content can cause mold to grow on your true morels. *Verpa* mushrooms are not common in the lower Midwest. In the upper Midwest they are called caps by those who pick and eat them.

Once, while we were teaching a weekend seminar and guided hunt in Michigan, the resort had to reschedule the cooks for our group. It seems they had overindulged in *Verpa* mushrooms while trying out new recipes and had been hospitalized. Both were in a coma.

Food tolerance varies. Avoidance is the best protection. If you accidentally pick a few and cook them with your other mushrooms, know that you will be OK, though you may experience a slightly drunk feeling. Any time you try a new variety of mushroom, especially wild ones, you should eat only a few and wait twenty-four hours. If you do not have an adverse reaction, eat more.

Beefsteak mushroom *(Gyromitra esculenta)*

4"–8" tall.

- Size varies greatly, especially in diameter.
- Rust to brown color with brain-like wrinkled cap.
- Irregularly shaped stems and caps.
- Insides are convoluted, with multiple walls and cottony lining.
- *Do not eat.* This mushroom is poisonous. It contains the chemical toxin monomethylhydrazine (MMH) which accumulates in the liver and can be fatal.

Elephant ear mushroom *(Gyromitra fastigiata)*

Vary in size and shape.

- Floppy saddle-shaped cap.
- Stems have multiple walls and cottony lining.
- Rust to brown colored.
- *Do not eat.* These false morels grow in the springtime in similar conditions to true morels.

Identification is simple: morels look like sea sponges and have hollow stems. *Verpa* mushrooms have cottony stems with caps that are joined to the stem at the top. *Gyromitra* mushrooms have dark rusty-colored caps and multiple-walled, cottony stems.

Stinkhorn mushrooms

This is not a true morel, nor is it categorized as a false morel, but it is sometimes confused with them. It grows in the fall. Morels are a springtime mushroom.

Stinkhorns are easy to identify by these distinct characteristics: First, true to their name, they stink. Second, their stems are like Styrofoam, and finally, the cap gets slimy as it is forming and only resembles the morel when flies have carried away the slime, revealing a pitted cap. They are best left alone; do not eat.

ODDITIES

As with any species there are subspecies of morels, such as unusually small varieties or large types. Morels from the burns look a bit different than their counterparts grown in other conditions. In addition to the usual varieties in the burns there is a type called a double-wall greenie. This type of morel has an inner lining that looks like a morel growing inside a morel. Often it is tan or moss colored. In 2002 we found double-wall greenies at seven thousand feet of elevation hunting the burns in Montana. In 2004 we found double-wall morels in four states in the Midwest, as well as Montana. We thought it was because of the unusually hard ground the morels adapted to break through. In 2010 the leaf litter was so impacted the same thing happened. The double-wall morels were similar in color to other morels growing nearby. Where we found black morels they were black, and where we found yellow morels they were yellow—but with a double wall.

We found another odd type of morel underneath the canopy of a dying sycamore tree in Missouri. They were seven of the most

Cup-sized morels found beneath a sycamore tree.

beautiful morels we have ever picked. They were so large they filled half a mesh collection bag by themselves. When we sliced them into ringlets to cook them, the walls were nearly an inch thick. They may have adapted the thick walls because they were growing from under very heavy bark that had fallen off the dying sycamore tree.

In Michigan we found morels growing in the gardens of the resort where we were doing a clinic. These little round jewels were mostly small. They looked like a cross between burn mushrooms and double-wall greenies. Many of them had pimply appendages between their ridges. The flavor was excellent. We were curious about the variety, but as long as we were able to identify them as morels, we didn't need a scientific identification once they hit the frying pan.

Morels do vary in size. We have found morels as little as less than half an inch tall and morels fourteen inches high. A friend in Iowa stumbled on an eighteen-inch-tall morel in the late season. Morels can grow in clusters too. Clusters are groups of morels that share a common mycelium strand and the stems are attached to each other. Friends in Michigan found a cluster of twenty-three morels; friends from Omaha found a cluster of twenty-seven in South Dakota; and while in Alaska burn hunting, we came across someone selling a cluster of over a hundred morels.

Morels are like snowflakes in that each and every one is unique. Part of the joy of the hunt is the challenge of finding them and noting their singularities. Like other sports, the more you know, the more you want to know. Some of the questions we still ponder are these: Why are some black morels round while others look like witches' hats? Why do morels seem to camouflage? Why do half-caps grow in groups? Why can't morels be filmed growing? Why are morels so hard to cultivate? Scientists are always making new discoveries; maybe one day they will answer our questions. For now, though, we'll have to settle for using what we do know and that is we love to hunt them, find them, and eat them. The rest of this book will help you do just that.

CHAPTER 3

Why Morels?

Spring is a beautiful time of year to be outdoors. The temperatures are generally mild, the air is fresh, the birds are singing, the foliage is bursting. It's a time of renewal, and the time when morels are growing.

Some people hunt morels to sell and some hunt morels because they are so good to eat, but a lot of people hunt morels because it's fun. Morel hunting is like a big Easter egg hunt. The hardest part—and greatest reward—is finding the mushrooms. Money and trophies are other rewards (some festivals have hunts and award trophies to the winners), but eating morels is reward enough.

SPORT

We play games while we mushroom hunt, the kind of game based on who is on the hunt. We start nearly every hunt with a game of "I spy." Whoever spots the first morel must cry out "I spy" so that everyone on the hunt can see that first one. Often we continue playing this for the first few mushrooms to help everyone on the hunt train their brains.

We have often heard stories from people who were walking in the woods and stopped to tinkle, smell a flower, or just rest a minute. As they looked around all of the sudden they saw mushrooms around them they hadn't seen before.

As you age your brain tunes out some information so you can focus on other things that are important to you. Your brain develops to protect you. If you don't like snakes, you notice everything that moves in the grass. If you don't like poison ivy, you notice every three-leaf plant. Likewise, if you don't like to fall, you notice every rock and tree root in your path. Until you train your brain to focus on the morel, you tune it out. Before the season starts, you should brain-train: Look at photographs or carvings of morels and focus on the importance of the morel.

Another game we play is naming the patches of morels within a social structure. When we find one morel we look for its big sister or brother. Sometimes we find twins; sometimes we find a little family; sometimes a neighborhood, town, or city, depending on the number of morels. This game is great for kids and teaches them the relationships between groups of people relative to amounts of things. Once our son yelled, "Look! There's New York City."

A friend of ours who likes to gamble created her own game, trying to guess the number of morels she would find. As she walks

Look, it's New York City.

through the woods and pretends to roll dice, she calls out for a seven, then a nine, and on up as she finds more and more morels. Morel hunting is surprisingly competitive. In our family we share them when it's time to eat them, but when we're in the woods we each want to find the biggest, the most, the biggest batch, the first, the most unusual, the largest cluster. When we do guided hunts we always acknowledge all of the hunters' finds, and when novice hunters find their very fist morels all by themselves, everyone stops to cheer. Though it's competitive, there can be great camaraderie in mushroom hunting, especially when you share.

To find out about organizations dedicated to morels and other mushrooms in your area or an area you are traveling to, contact:

North American Mycological Association (NAMA)
10 Lynn Brooke Place
Charleston, West Virginia 25312-9521
www.namyco.org

On the internet, you can find out about groups, guides, and events across the country and beyond. Type in "morel" and a plethora of information is at your fingertips. Just beware that information is not regulated on the internet. Most important, use caution if you are going to purchase morels, particularly fresh morels.

It's a joy to be in the woods and everyone who hunts is a winner. As we said in the beginning of this chapter, the biggest challenge in morel hunting is finding the morels and it is reward enough to enjoy several skillets full.

FLAVOR

Eating morels is a sport all its own. If you love to eat mushrooms you are a mycophagist, and in Russia they have a special name for people who are crazy for mushrooms: raszh (pronounced "rash"). It's no wonder people are raszh: Morels taste like sirloin steak. That alone makes them a worthy target to hunt. They are in the same family as truffles, which may explain why their flavor is so outstanding.

Tasty little morsels.

We like to compare the different varieties of morels using the same language as is used in wine tasting. Black morels have a deep, full-bodied flavor. Depending on the woods they come from or the types of trees in the area where they are picked, they smell and taste like the soft sweetness of cherry, maple, and sycamore trees. Likewise, under oak leaves, ash trees, and near hickory, they have a distinct nuttiness. Long-stemmed half-caps have surprisingly big flavor. They don't bread well because of their delicate texture, but they are light, moist, and sweet no matter where they grow. They are often found in large quantities and are good for flavoring meats (see the chapter on preparing morels).

The tight, small, gray morels have a distinct earthy freshness to them and are good marinated. Little grays turn into big grays with a little patience. These make the best sautéed morels because they are firm, usually thick, and taste like steak.

Yellow morels *(esculenta)* have the best texture and a robust, steaklike flavor. Small yellow morels look like peanuts; they are warm-weather morels and usually grow quickly.

The great big morels found at the end of the season *(crassipes)* are best prepared like onion rings—cut into ringlets, breaded, and fried. They are also great stuffed. Their texture is thinner but the robust morel flavor comes through.

Morels themselves have very few calories, unless you cook them in butter. They have few vitamins and are very low in carbohydrates and fats. Besides their wonderful flavor, morels are a good source of minerals (especially iron) and proteins, although you should not substitute them for other protein sources in your diet. Worldwide, and especially in China, mushrooms are studied and used for medicinal purposes. They may help the body absorb antioxidants. The false morel *Verpa* mushroom has been studied for its muscle relaxant quality. There is much to learn about all mushrooms, and in order for them to survive and thrive, all mushroom hunters should use mesh collection bags (see chapter 6). This simple collection bag will insure that morel mushrooms spore and propagate, continuing the mushroom's life cycle for the joy of eating them, for the health of the woods, and for medicinal purposes yet to be discovered.

CHAPTER 4

When to Look for Morels

TEMPERATURES

Mushroom hunters know that spring is the peak season for mushroom hunting. Cars are parked along roadsides, woods are full, and secrecy abounds. But what knowledgeable mushroom hunters know is that watching the calendar or waiting for the weekend just doesn't work. So how do you know when to start looking for morels? In conjunction with spring (when the trees start to bud), start checking likely spots when the daytime temperatures have stayed above fifty-five for at least five days after a week without a frost. The morels may not be there yet—it generally takes two weeks after the last frost for the morels to show up—but you want to be the first to find them. Check every three of four days until you start seeing them. Black morels are the first variety to come up. Once the cycle starts, they will continue to come up even if temperatures fall. In northern states, many people have reported finding morels coming up through the snow or surviving freezes.

One Memorial Day weekend in the northwest triangle of Minnesota on the Canadian border, we encountered unusually cool temperatures while mushroom hunting. Only one day was above fifty degrees (daily temperatures are normally in the sixties then). Previously the area had warm temperatures and a tremendous amount of rain. With temperatures in the mid-forties we hunted high ground and south- and west-facing slopes, and picked hun-

The perfect woods ... deep leaf liter, trees with gray bark, the height of spring.

dreds of black morels. The season had started and the morels had to reproduce. The temperatures did not reduce the number of morels, and most of the morels we found were three and four inches tall.

We arrived in Montana on June 13 with four to six inches of snow on the ground. The morels had begun to grow—we have the pictures to prove it!

Generally, black morels grow in open sunny spots in the woods when the daytime temperatures are in the low sixties. Half-cap morels like daily temperatures in the mid-sixties and grow in open sunny areas of the woods. You'll typically find gray morels under the canopy of trees, often at the bases of trees, when daytime temperatures are in the high sixties. Yellow morels like seventy-degree daytime temperatures and the shaded areas of the tree canopy. Big foot mushrooms are the last of the season, appearing when daily temperatures are in the high seventies. They are most often found

Surviving the snow.

in grassy areas, heavy shade, and low areas near water. Usually when this variety is up the grass is quite tall. It can make finding them a chore, but you can spot them from a good distance when the ground cover is low. New batches stop producing when the daytime temperatures reach eighty for a few days. There are always cool spots in the woods like deep ravines and heavily shaded north-facing hills. These are the areas where morels will be at the tail end of the season.

The season ends when the morels have deteriorated or they have all been picked. Some years the hunting season can last four to six weeks. Further north the hunting season lasts longer because of the naturally cooler temperatures. In the Midwest seasons can be as short as one to two weeks. That makes for a very long time until the next hunting season unless you become a mushroom chaser and start following the mushrooms north.

Spring follows the sun in relationship to the Earth's rotation, and as the daytime temperatures rise, the morels fruit, moving northward at about a hundred miles a week. Mushroom hunters in Texas and Georgia start picking morels in March, but in Michigan the peak season for white morels is May. In mountainous areas where the higher elevations are cooler, the same principles apply. Similarly, the temperatures in the valleys warm up early in spring, and as spring progresses into summer, the warm temperatures move up the mountain. We picked morels the third week of August at an elevation of seven thousand feet.

Temperatures are the key to knowing where to start the search. Hunt logically. In the cool, early part of the season, morels are in the sunnier, warmer locations, typically south- and west-facing slopes or flat areas between the canopy of the trees. Black morels and half-cap morels tend to grow in open areas, starting on south-facing slopes, then west, east, and finally on the north. If you look up in these open areas you will notice an opening in the tree canopy and a lot of sky.

As spring progresses, keep track of the weather conditions the previous days and nights. Morels are adaptable and they grow initially at night, so if the evening temperatures are hot, morels might be on the east-facing hillsides or near the shade of pine trees. If the temperatures drop, morels are likely to be on sunny hilltops or south-facing slopes. If you become an area hunter (more in chapter 7) and keep your eyes focused on the ground, you're going to see a pattern—morels will grow in similar places throughout the woods. You will find more mushrooms by looking for the pattern and then repeating it throughout the woods. If the woods haven't been hunted or disturbed for several days there will be overlapping fruitings or patterns there.

The gray and yellow morels, which appear when daily temperatures reach the high sixties to mid seventies, follow the same progression. They will start coming up on the warm south-facing slopes, then west-facing slopes, east-facing, and last, north-facing slopes. Whether by natural habit or because of the warmer temperatures, these varieties of morels are almost directly under the canopy of trees. By this time the trees start to leaf out, which creates dappled shade. Foliage development occurs in relationship to sunlight and how long the days are—you can track it on a gardener's plant hardiness zone calendar. Morels, however, develop based on temperatures, so it is hard to place a date on the season or make connections between morel growth and other plant growth or tree foliage. We have heard everything from when the dandelions are in all phases to when the lilacs bloom. The only real common denominator is that these events all take place in the spring.

A gardener's plant hardiness zone chart can show you the average last frost for an area. If you move or travel, you can use this indicator to check the local zone and use it as a starting point. There are a few internet sites that track the path of the morel too. One thing is sure: morels come up on their time, not when you have a day off or on the weekend.

Morel hunts become finds when you know what the daily temperatures have been and use a little common sense. Think like a morel: if it gets too warm, it grows in the shade, if it gets too cool, it grows in sunny spots.

SIGNS

For many mushroom hunters, a hot day after a rain, when daily temperatures are in the mid to high seventies, is their sign to start mushroom hunting. This group of people, and there are a lot of them, miss much of the morel mushroom season. Because the rain will make the mushrooms larger (morels are more than ninety percent water), they will be easier to see. This type of mushroom hunter will find some grays but mostly yellows and big foots. They will miss all the flavor delight that the black and half-cap mushrooms have.

In central Iowa many people start looking on tax day, April 15. Others believe that when the mayapples are blooming, it's time to mushroom hunt. We've even heard a theory that the mushrooms grow when the moon is full. In Minnesota and Michigan, many believe that Mother's Day weekend is the best time to hunt mushrooms.

The best sign to know when to hunt morels is to know the approximate time frame for the arrival of spring in your area. Start observing the temperatures a few weeks before the last frost, and pay close attention. When there hasn't been a frost for at least a week and the daytime temperatures have been in the high fifties to low sixties for five days, check a few likely spots. Spend about fifteen minutes in an area, walking at a quick pace. If the mushrooms are up, you'll see them. If they aren't up yet, you probably haven't missed them. Check every three or four days, rotating spots. Once the mushrooms start to come up, your window of opportunity is as long or short as the temperatures allow. Go every three or four days to pick new batches, again rotating spots.

CHAPTER 5

Where to Hunt for Morels

Where do mushrooms grow? Anywhere spore falls back to the ground.

Morels have been found growing up through rocks, along railroad tracks, in pine needles, coming up through snow, next to an inner-city swing set, deep in a forest, in a meadow, in old orchards, in the laboratory, and in city dumps. None of these conditions sound similar.

Each morel has 250,000 to 500,000 spores in its cap. The morel is the reproductive part of the underground organism. The fruit that we eat—the morel mushroom—starts growing at night when the temperatures and moisture-level are just right. When exposed to the sun, it begins to dry out. As it dries out, it begins expelling the tiny dust-like spore into the air. The spore becomes airborne and falls back to the ground to start the process again. To aid morel reproduction, all mushroom hunters should use a mesh collection bag (see chapter 6). The morels air-dry in the bag as you carry it. The mesh also allows the spore to escape, becoming airborne and falling back to the ground. Carrying your morels in mesh bags will increase the morel population.

Have you ever stepped on or kicked a puffball? The puff is spore. You can see spore from a morel by drying the mushroom and letting the yellow spore accumulate. The pattern that develops is like a photo negative of the ridges as the spore comes out of the pits.

Looking east through the opening in the canopy, black morels start appearing on the south-facing slopes to the left in these ideal woods. As it warms up, they start coming up on the north-facing hillside on the right. Then half-cap morels start showing up on the south-facing hill, and so on through each variety.

Whatever direction the wind naturally blows in a hunting area will affect where the morels will grow in the future.

If you found morels on the top of a hill in the past, look down-hill and downwind. Spore is very sticky. Typically, spore will get caught in tall grasses or get stuck in the mud along damp areas, remaining close to where it was released. We've used mesh bags for years and hunted grounds where mesh bags have been used for years, and we find the results of using them—lots of morels—up and down the trails and right near parking spots.

The most natural environments for morel mushrooms are hard-wood forests and heavily wooded areas, particularly woods with trees having white to gray bark. Remember, the morel is the first responder to feed on the decay of the root material of a dying tree.

It also feeds off the debris on the forest floor. Keep in mind the differences between the varieties of morels, which influence where each will likely grow, as well as daily temperatures, which affect the side of the hill the morels might be on.

Morels are not as fond of trees that produce nuts and acorns as they are of other trees, but if those are the only trees in your area, morels may be there. For instance, the Ozarks are dominated by oak trees, over two hundred varieties of them. Morels can be found there. Morels favor some oak tree varieties more than others: the gray morel can be found under or near white oaks in southern Missouri.

Morels can be found in other places, but it's hard to look for morels where there are no natural indicators. You might find them in a meadow if the meadow lies between the car and the woods and the wind blows from the woods. The spore have likely blown out of the woods, caught in the tall grass of the meadow, and reproduced there.

Morels are often found near railroad tracks that cut through woods. Typically the track is built on a rise. The spores from morels in the woods become airborne, flow through the open area, and stick to the hump that supports the track. When limbs are trimmed to clear the track, the underground root material associated with them decays, providing good conditions for morels to grow. Be sure to hunt the edges of the woods nearby as well as the open area.

Morels are often found in old orchards. When the fruit trees get old and start to die, you will find morels. The fallen fruit and pruning are other reasons the orchards are good for finding morels.

If you own your own land, read the chapter on scouting to help you determine the best places to search on your property. If you don't own your own land or you like to chase morels, hunt on public land. Most game hunters are familiar with Department of Natural Resources (DNR) land, public land that is regulated state by state, and mushroom hunters should be too. (See chapter 14 for a contact list of state and federal agencies that regulate public land.)

For city parks, college campuses, or other local areas, use your phone book or internet for contact information. Having permission to hunt is better than getting a fine and having your days' work taken from you.

To sum up, hunt anywhere with a likely food source (root material of dying trees, shrubs, and woody plants) and plenty of moisture to help the morels grow. Look for woods with trees with white to gray bark, gray leaf litter, and trees of all ages. Old trees die and not all young trees survive due to competition for water, nutrients, and sunshine. Both provide a food source for morels. You can ask a mushroom hunter about the trees, but asking where to hunt is taboo.

Spring is short, so look in the most likely places. Hunt the woods with the best chance of finding morels.

It's helpful to keep records with information on each hunt, such as the day's weather conditions, the prior weeks' weather, the wind direction, what the winter and spring in general were like, maps of the locations, and pounds picked. Morels have a short season. With records like this you will be prepared with areas to hunt with known success. Our advice on where to hunt: head for the woods and keep your eyes open. You will find morels.

CHAPTER 6

Preparing to Hunt

MESH COLLECTION BAG

"Do you want more mushrooms? Do you?" That was the question our friend Larry Lonik, "the Mushroom Man," posed in his video *Motherlode*. John posed the question to Larry while cooking morels for us. It was so simple and to the point. Everyone who loves morels wants more. It became our mantra. Larry Lonik was part of a select group of men that grew morel mushrooms for commercial sales. It was short-lived but his laboratory work made him realize that collecting morels in buckets, bags, and sacks eliminated spores. Not only that, plastic bags suffocate morels with heat and humidity. But even if the produce remained safe, the spores had no way to get out, to reproduce.

Morels collected in a mesh bag air-dry and release spore that escapes through the mesh and falls back to the forest floor to make morels for future generations. Spore that gets trapped in the fibers of the mesh will remain fertile from hunt to hunt and season to season. You become the Johnny Appleseed of the morels, and the morels you harvest have a chance to reproduce.

Also, morels kept in plastic bags deteriorate rapidly due to the heat and humidity within the hollow specimen. Morels in a mesh bag breathe, air-dry, and stay much fresher.

This is the only piece of equipment essential to mushroom hunting. We recommend using a bag designed specifically for morel

A bag full of mushrooms.

mushroom hunting. Team Morel's Sporebag, for example, is a cloth mesh collection bag with a carrier pocket on the side, designed with a wide bottom to keep the morels from being crushed. The fabric mesh is gentler on morels than plastic mesh. Bags like this can be used for many years. The attached storage pocket allows the mesh bag to be rolled up and stored between hunts and seasons. Do not wash your bags. Spore that gets trapped in the fibers can stay fertile from hunt to hunt and season to season, and may be released at another time to further morel reproduction. You become the Johnny Appleseed for the morels. Any similar cloth mesh collection bag will do as long as it has these same features and is kept dry and protected between hunts. Using a mesh collection bag will also keep your morels fresh so that the produce on your dinner table is at its best.

The morel population has been declining for years. Stories say morels were picked by the bushel fifty years ago. The science of how morels grow was not known and spores were trapped in collection bags, reducing the morel population. If all mushroom

Carry several mesh bags and collect half-caps in a separate bag so their higher moisture content does not mold your other varieties.

hunters begin using mesh bags, we can reverse this downward trend. Walking an extra half hour in the woods can make a difference too. Morels cycle so it takes a few years to see the difference, but when you do it is so exciting. Our first experience with this was in southern Illinois. We hunted all day in the state forest, picking hundreds of mushrooms, quitting only when we became aware of the late hour and the two-mile hike back to the car. On the trail back to the car we found lots of mushrooms right along the path. When we reached the makeshift parking lot, we found more morels right by the cars. Our host laughed as he explained his ploy: he took us in the opposite direction than most of the mushroom hunters so that upon our return we would see for ourselves the results of using mesh collection bags.

Another reason to use mesh collection bags is that morels are not yet available fresh year-round at grocery stores. In some states it is against the law to sell fresh morels in grocery stores, even in season. Dried morels that are sold in grocery stores grow wild and are still collected by hand. You can help the morel population by using a mesh collection bag and spreading spore.

You can even help morels grow where you would like them to grow. Here's how: every spring, collect morel mushrooms in your mesh bag and carry them to the area where you would like morels to grow. The conditions should be similar to the mushroom's natural growing conditions, say, in woods close to your home or in an area of the backyard with leaf litter and debris. Carry them around in the bag in this area for half an hour. The longer you walk around letting the morels dry out, the more spores you release. Drink a cup of coffee, a soda, or a beer—make it enjoyable. If you have used the bag several times, you also have residue spore that may be released. You can't plant morels in a specific spot, nor can you control where they will come up. The underground organism feeds on dying trees and debris, so if a tree dies two yards away in your suburban neighborhood, the underground morel system will develop to the location of the food, and the fruiting body, the morel, will grow there. You can nurture an area to produce morels for future hunts by spreading spores in that area; just make sure it has dying trees and shrubs to support the underground organism.

In Omaha, Nebraska, Kevin Townsend dries his morels on his back deck. The breeze carries the spore away from the house and into the yard, he now has a few morels growing along the fence line where he mulches heavily.

It takes approximately ten thousand spores to make another morel. We need to do everything we can to help morels reproduce. In nature, spore becomes airborne from the morel on the ground. We can improve upon Mother Nature by carrying the morels around the woods in

Grow your own morels: Dry morels in an area you want morels to grow. Spore will become airborne and fall back to the ground.

mesh bags, not only helping the spore get airborne but spreading spore throughout the woods and potentially into new areas of woods. Understanding that the spore needs to get airborne will help you look for morels in unlikely places; think about why morels are in such scattered locations.

Mesh collection bags are essential equipment for a mushroom hunter. Do you want more mushrooms? Do you?

CLOTHING AND ACCESSORIES

We grew up playing in the woods. Between hunting, camping, and fishing we learned how to dress for the woods, much of which carries over to morel hunting. Practical clothing, shoes, hat, and gear make a day in the woods most enjoyable.

In the spring, bugs are just waking up from a long winter's nap, and they are hungry. When deer hunters go into the woods, they try to be as neutral smelling as possible so the deer won't smell them. For morel hunters it is a matter of smelling neutral so as not to attract annoying bugs, especially flies and mosquitoes. Don't use lotion, perfume, or hair products when you are going mushroom hunting. Ticks are attracted to body heat, so wear light colors that reflect the sun's heat and help keep the body cool. You can use bug repellant, but another way to keep the bugs away is to cut laundry dryer sheets into strips and tuck them around your ankles, neckline, and cuffs. Ticks and mosquitoes will not cross the chemical barrier. The scent doesn't matter, and you can even use unscented ones. This method is safe for children, and you can keep the sheets in a plastic baggie to reuse them.

Always wear a hat with a brim in the woods. Not only will it shade you from the sun, but when you are looking at the ground it is easy to brush by limbs, and the brim of the hat will protect your eyes.

You also need a good pair of hiking boots for rough terrain, ankle-high boots for hilly or mountainous areas, or comfortable walking shoes for open or flat areas. Hiking socks help too: they give support and wick moisture from your feet. Be practical. Tennis shoes are made for sports and for hard surfaces like gyms and black-top, whereas hiking shoes and boots are made for rough terrain. Tree thorns can penetrate tennis shoes. The right footwear will also help prevent twisted ankles.

Because good mushroom hunting land is full of brambles, gooseberries, wild roses, and raspberry bushes, we recommend brush busters, a type of nylon-faced hunting pant that doesn't tear easily. Wear a T-shirt with a long-sleeved shirt over it. The long-sleeved shirt will protect your arms from the thorns and bugs, and if the weather is warm, you can take the outer shirt off to cool down. Layering is also a better strategy for changing weather conditions.

You should also carry a pack with essentials such as water, tissues, an energy bar, medicines, first-aid items, lip balm, a monocular, GPS, walkie–talkie, and camera. Pack for your particular needs. We also carry a fish scale to measure how many pounds an area produces; we weigh the morels fresh-picked.

The mushroom hunting rule of thumb is walk a mile, pick a pound. That takes time. When it comes to clothing and supplies, remember, the more comfortable you are the more likely you will stay in the woods all day, pick more mushrooms, and enjoy the experience.

SAFETY

Keep in mind when dressing for the woods, whether you're hunting public ground or private land, that morel season is often turkey season as well. Know what the regulations are where you are going. Regulations for turkey hunting vary state to state. Even if you think there won't be any hunters on the land where you will be hunting, prepare yourself, and be aware. Safety should be your number one concern. Turkey hunters in some states must unload their guns or leave the woods by a certain time of day. In Missouri, hunters must be out of the woods by 1:00 p.m., but in nearby states the hunters can hunt dawn to dusk. Most states do not allow hunting in state parks, but DNR lands, some Corps of Engineers lands, and some forestry lands do have regulated turkey seasons.

Many states are revising their regulations as turkey populations increase. See chapter 14 for phone numbers and websites to check for the most up-to-date information.

Accidents occur every season. Stay safe, and follow the guidelines set by the turkey hunter safety classes. W. W. "Bill" Willis of the Grand Valley Chapter of the National Wild Turkey Federation sent us the following guidelines:

First, avoid the colors of the American flag: do not wear red, white, or blue because turkey's heads are the target and they are red, white, and blue. Blue jeans are *not* safe in turkey woods! Do not wear black or dark brown. Wear khakis; not only is it a safe color, it reflects the sunlight, so you'll stay cooler. And because the color is light, it will be much easier to see a tick crawling up your leg. Avoid white T-shirts and white socks.

If you see a hunter, do not wave. Sit or stand motionless. If a gun is pointed in your direction, shout or whistle. Turkey hunters are after turkeys, not mushroom hunters. Check what the turkey hunting regulations are where you hunt. States regulate shot loads individually, and the smaller the number, the more lethal the load is. States now require safety courses for young hunters, generally preteens, but most hunting accidents are caused by hunters thirty-nine and older who have been grandfathered in to the law.

Many mushroom hunters are not aware of turkey season, and a lot of turkey hunters who look for morels after they are done turkey hunting while still wearing their camouflage often think they are the only ones in the woods. Be aware of your surroundings.

Some mushroom hunters want to keep their hunting areas secret and may not want to be seen in the woods. They wear camouflage to disguise their whereabouts. We know many morel hunters go to the woods just this one time of year and may not be aware of turkey hunters. We printed our mushroom hunting T-shirts on safety orange and safety yellow with them in mind. Bright-colored shirts will help others know you are in the woods.

Some of these same hunters are not aware that crossing purple-sprayed trees means they have crossed onto private land and that the purple means "keep out."

If everyone follows the safety rules, has the right gear, and takes the time to walk around with their morels in their mesh bag to release spore back into the environment, we will all have a great time, morels will become more abundant, and everyone will benefit from the fungi becoming more abundant in nature.

THE LOOK

"The look" is about how to look for mushrooms, not how you look while mushroom hunting. Try this exercise to understand how distance affects the shape you see: stretch your arm out, make a fist, and put your thumb up. Look at your thumb. You can see your fist and a perfect outline of your thumb. Now pull your arm in to your stomach and look down at your thumb. Now you can only see the tip of your thumb with your finger wrapped around it. Clearly distance affects how you view the target. While walking in the woods, you will more easily spot the shape of the morel out in front of you, rather than at your feet.

While hunting for morels, look for the unusual texture of the morel as well as its shape. Often this unusual texture will stand out from the background before you actually see the morel. Brain-train before the season starts: look at morels; memorize the shapes and textures. It will make them easier to spot when you go hunting.

Look into the distance, spot the shape, the texture, and then identify the morel. Once you find one, stop. Usually you will find more, so take the time to look around. Was it a dying tree that kicked up the morel there? Walk in a spiral around the tree, all the way to the edges of the branches. Go back in the opposite direction. Look at the ground from all directions, from all heights; often other morels look like shadows. If you're in a group everyone can help look for more mushrooms. Usually if you find one morel, especially a black or half-cap morel, others are nearby.

The person who doesn't like snakes is always the one to notice them; the person who worries about poison ivy is the one who notices all the three-leaf foliage. Their brains are protecting them from these threats as they walk. Less important information fades into the background. Stopping often is a valuable technique for mushroom hunting. When you stand still, the brain is no longer in protective walking mode, and you can see detail you did not see before. When you walk through an area, stop and turn around, and you may see morels where you did not see them before. The mushrooms were there, but you didn't notice them. The whole notion of morels popping out of the ground came from this kind of experience.

When you find a morel, look around the immediate environment and determine what triggered the morel to grow there. If the trigger is a dying tree on a south-facing slope, look for all the dying trees on south-facing slopes. If the area is open, ten feet down the north side of a hill, look for all the similar areas facing the same direction, ten feet down the hillsides. This is called a pattern. Search the woods for similar patterns, and you will find more mushrooms. Use a compass or GPS or the direction of the sun to help identify these patterns. We don't yet understand why morel production in nature is so varied, but morels are very selective toward temperatures, moisture, and food source. If you follow a pattern throughout the woods, you can cover more ground more successfully. If you are hunting in woods that no one has hunted for a week and the weather pattern hasn't changed, you will discover several overlapping patterns playing out, and you will find more mushrooms. Remember, morels grow nightly through the season. One night may be chilly, triggering the morels to grow in the sunny spots. The next night may be much warmer, causing the morels to grow in the shade. Keep track of the nighttime weather conditions for the previous few days and look for morels in likely areas. Keep your eyes open, repeat the pattern, and pick lots of mushrooms.

CHAPTER 7

Scouting for Morels

It's not certain that when you go mushroom hunting you will actually find morels—or is it? Like other sports it takes practice, planning, the right gear, and knowledge to be successful.

You have learned about the types of morels and their habits, we've covered the proper gear, and we've explained the need for a mesh collection bag, but how do you practice a sport that has such a short season? Learn to scout for likely areas, record information, and practice. There isn't a time of year that we aren't thinking about morels. Because we chase morels, teach classes in morel hunting, and guide every year, we get a lot of practice. We also scout areas to determine if morels will be there, and you can learn to do this too.

LOCATION, LOCATION, LOCATION

We scout for good areas to hunt year round. As we are traveling, we examine the woods from the roadside and determine whether we think it would be good for morel hunting. We use a journal to keep hunt and weather information, we track likely locations with descriptions of why we think they might be good. Keep in mind trees with white to gray bark, nearby water sources, and the appearance of leaf litter. With this information we can predetermine whether morels will be there, and so can you.

Because the morel mushroom season in any area is short, hunt smart. Observe your surroundings. If you don't own your own

Trees are easier to find than morels.

land, be a good steward so that you will be welcomed back, and be ethical wherever you hunt. There is plenty of public ground, even in cities. (See chapter 14 for a list of resources of public land.) Wherever you go, ask permission, know the rules, carry out whatever you carry in, and use a mesh collection bag.

To begin scouting, choose up to ten areas within half an hour from your home or work. Keep a map with your journal, and highlight the locations. These can be parks, drainage areas, easements, schools, new construction, or any place with trees. If you own land or can travel farther out to the country, follow the same method. Observe the areas year round. In late summer look for trees showing signs of stress or beginning to die. The foliage will yellow and fall very early. The bark may be cracked or falling, with signs of rust or other fungi. As fall approaches, look for woods with yellow and purple leaves dominating early, followed by red to bright orange leaves. These are the elm, poplar, cottonwood, sycamore, aspen, and birch trees, followed by the maple, ash, and hawthorn trees. In the winter months notice the number of trees with white bark—the poplar, cottonwood, sycamore, and birch trees. The areas with trees that still have leaves, typically rust-colored leaves, are woods with a lot of oak trees, which are typically not as conducive to finding morels.

FOOD AND WATER

Remember, morels are a fungus, and the job of fungus in nature is to decompose dying material. The dying material is the food source for the underground organism. Fungi are essential to healthy woods. Along with termites, carpenter ants, and a few other insects, the fungi break down wood and return the nutrients to the soil. When scouting for potential morel hunting areas, look for a few signs.

The morel's food source is the primary concern. First, look for woods with a high percentage of elm, poplar, aspen, birch, ash, maple, and sycamore trees. As you walk in the woods, look for gray leaf litter. The leaves from these types of trees fall early in the season and have a long winter to break down. These same trees also have falling or peeling bark and drop little branches and seedpods. All of this is food for morels. As discussed, the main food source is the root material of a dying tree, and when part of the tree dies above ground, an equal amount of root material below ground dies. Larger trees provide a greater food source to the underground organism, giving it more energy to grow more morels. Every variety of morel grows best when there is thick gray leaf litter. Uniquely, the gray and yellow morel varieties somewhat camouflage to the color of the leaf litter even though they are two distinct varieties. Morels are over ninety percent water, so look for a water source nearby too. The water source will be an indicator of the quality of morels you will find in an area. When water tables are up, the morels that season are larger. Look for creeks, ponds, runoff areas, and so on. Record this information for each area throughout the seasons. When spring is near, check the most likely areas. Start early and take a quick fifteen-minute walk in the woods. If the morels are up, you'll spot them. If the area doesn't look as promising as you had hoped, remove it from your search list. Not only will you be among the first to find morels in the spring, you'll have several places to look when you have a little time. Rotate where you look so you can capture several batches of morels throughout the spring. At the end of your hunts, record your successes, the date, weather conditions of the previous few days, and wind direction. As you write all this down, think about why the morels were in one area rather than another. Expand your spots to similar areas, and remove unsuccessful areas from your list. Over the years you can refer back to the information in your journal to hone your skills. Make the best use of your mushroom hunting time during the short season by scouting areas well ahead of the season and searching the areas most likely to produce morels.

TEMPERATURE

Start going to your spots early, because you might find morels earlier than you would think. Black morels *(antigusticeps)* come out surprisingly early. In Minnesota, we've picked black morels in 45- to 55-degree temperatures. The season had been triggered by a week of warm temperatures without a frost, followed by cool rains. The pattern was high ground, sunny knolls, and south- and west-facing hillsides. Check every three to four days. You will be the first in your area to know when the morels are up, and you will be able to pick several crops as the morels progress through the different varieties as the temperatures rise. Remember, a full week without a frost and then four or five days with the daytime temperatures in the high fifties to low sixties will bring out the black morels. With about every five-degree increase in daily temperatures the other varieties follow: the half-cap morels, gray morels, yellows, and finally the big foots, which complete the season when the temperatures rise to the mid-eighty degrees for a few days.

Learn as much as you can about morel behavior, get the right gear, and scout. If you plan to chase morels, apply the same scouting principals. Morels move north about one hundred miles a week with local conditions affecting the duration of growth. Take a quick fifteen-minute walk in a new woods looking for the signs of good morel hunting grounds: the right kinds of trees, gray leaf litter, dying or stressed trees, and a water source. If these signs are there, the morels will likely be there too. Then determine the pattern and follow it, keeping your eyes open for multiple patterns and multiple batches of morels.

MORE TIPS

Avoid areas dominated by locust trees, iron wood, or hedge row, as well as woods dominated by nut- and acorn-producing trees.

You can use local fishing websites to get the local temperatures for lakeside mushroom hunting. You can access satellite imaging to preview woods and forests to visualize areas to hunt. You can develop your own tricks for being in the right place at the perfect temperature.

CHAPTER 8

Hunting Techniques

TREE HUNTING VERSUS AREA HUNTING

Some people simply go for a walk in the woods hoping to find morels, while experienced hunters use one of two basic techniques: tree hunting and area hunting. Typically, tree hunters are looking for dead elm trees where they mostly find gray and yellow morels. Dutch elm disease arrived in the Midwest in the 1970s and nearly wiped out the elm trees. Morels were abundant. How morels grow was not known at that time, and the mushrooms were collected in bread bags. In areas where native elm trees still exist, elm tree hunting is a simple way to collect morels. However, much of the spore that makes new mushrooms was eliminated by using plastic bags. We now know to use mesh collection bags and to hunt many varieties of dying trees.

By contrast, area hunters start out by choosing woods that are likely to have morels, checking for gray leaf litter and scouring the ground in search of morels. This technique for hunting morels works best with a group of hunters. Line up about fifteen feet apart and walk in the same direction. As you walk, look for morels and when someone has a good find, use everyone in the group to locate all the morels in that immediate area. When we chase morels and visit unfamiliar woods, we begin by looking for ideal areas. Depending on the variety of morel that is up and the pattern we find that day, we sometimes switch from area hunting to tree hunting for morels.

When black morels and half-cap morels are up, it is much easier to work as a team. These two varieties appear first in open areas and are spread out. You find one, and while you are picking it, you see another. In Minnesota we found an area with many poplar and birch trees that had been clear-cut years earlier. We started from the parking lot, working out and over the area in a pie shape. Each time we worked our way back to the car with full bags of morels. We spent seven hours hunting this area and picked seven full bags of morels, ten to fourteen pounds each.

With death comes new life.

In southern Illinois one year the half-cap morels were like weeds. We didn't stop the car unless we could pick a bag full. The ground was black and white with caps and stems. We covered a lot of areas without needing to think about the particular species of trees.

Another time, we were area hunting in Michigan with a group when it became clear that on that day most of the black morels were fitting a specific pattern based on three-trunk cherry trees. Trees with one or more of the trunks decaying produced a one- to two-pound batch of morels, depending on the size of the tree. Every tree that fit that scenario had morels. That day we were tree hunters.

Look in the open areas of the woods.

The tree provides the food source for the underground organism of the morel. Remember, the most important tip for mushroom finding is that morels are the first responders to feed on the decay of the root material of dying trees. Morels also feed on roots of woody shrubs that are dying and annual decay from plants like snake grass and ferns. Morels grow abundantly when there has been a fire, flood, or bulldozing because while the trees and other vegetation above ground is destroyed, the root material underground remains in place and becomes a food fest for fungi. The food source provides enough energy for every underground organism to shoot up morels to reproduce. The underground organism may also sense its existence threatened in this kind of situation and reproduce for the survival of the species. Knowing about the relationship of morels to trees can help you determine when area hunting is best and when tree hunting is best.

We are area hunters first. The advantage to this method is that our eyes are on the ground where morels grow, not in the treetops searching for dying trees. As described in chapter 1, the black, half-cap, and big foot morel varieties grow in more open areas of the woods, not directly associated with the trees. Black morels and half-caps grow when the leaves are barely on the trees and the daily temperatures are cool. They are found where the ground warms up first—in the open areas between the canopy. When area hunting for big foot morels, we look for tall grass and wet areas, as big foots are the hot temperature morels that like cooler spots. The gray and yellow varieties of morels are more directly associated with the trees, but if you start out area hunting and recognize a strong pattern, it is easy to switch hunting methods. In the frying pan all varieties of morels are delicious, so we don't want to leave any behind.

Teaming up to tree hunt can work well when one person acts as a tree spotter and the others search the ground around the chosen trees. The spotter need only look for dying trees. In the early part of the season, before the leaves come on, look for trees with cracks or peeling bark, with or without signs of rusts or other fungi. As the season progresses, the trees not getting their leaves are the trees that are dying.

FINDING MORELS BY THE TREE

Morels, especially the gray and early yellow varieties, are found in woods that have trees with mainly white to gray bark. These are primarily deciduous trees that have a root system that is spread out, and often the root material will be noticeable at ground level. These same tree types lose their leaves early in the fall. Some scientists believe there is a symbiotic relationship between the morel organism and the roots of trees, meaning there is environmental communication as well as an exchange of food, water, and nutrients. This relationship can go on for years without noticeable morel mushroom activity. Then when the tree becomes distressed or begins to die, morels grow abundantly, having the most morels the first year of distress, the second year about half as many, and the third year fewer, if any. The morel organism produces a lot of morels (the fruit) to give it the best chance of reproducing, and the decaying root material gives the underground morel organism plenty of food for the energy to do this job. The number of morels under a dying tree is proportionate to the size and type of tree. Small dying trees will have fewer morels than older, larger trees.

You'll find more morels if you understand the relationship between trees and morels. Trees are big indicators of where to look for morels in the vastness of the forest—it is much easier to find a tree than a morel. Rather than run from tree to tree looking for morels, spot some trees that are dying and area hunt between the dying trees.

Once you have chosen woods that have trees with white to gray bark, good leaf litter, and plenty of moisture, look for signs of trees that are stressed or dying. When you look into the canopy, observe the leaves, and look for a tree whose leaves do not look like the others, the tree not getting its leaves on when others are. Maybe the tree was struck by lightning and only half of it is dying. Maybe the tree is infested with bugs and all the leaves are small and furled. When you get closer to the wounded tree, see if it has slipping bark. Splits and cracks in the bark indicate trees in the first phase of dying, which equates to large numbers of morels, depending on the size of the tree. By the time the bark is stripped the tree is past the prime season for fruiting morels but may still have some morels nearby. As long as the tree is still standing and has some bark, it is worth checking. Once the root material is sufficiently decomposed, the tree will fall over. Until this happens there is root material to decay and be used as food for mushrooms.

The following information describes specific tree types and how they relate to morel fruitings. Understanding this will help you find more morels.

Elm Trees

Eastern Nebraska, parts of Iowa, upper Illinois, and southern Wisconsin are famous for morels found under elm trees. The Dutch elm disease ravaged our country in the 1970s, the so-called heyday of morel picking. Today, there are not as many old, native elm trees as there once were and not as many so large as to have the quantities of fruiting morels as in the past. The places that have replacement elm trees, younger trees that have grown since the infestation, are great to hunt. The elm trees grow at the edges of the woods, so they are easy to spot from the road if you know what to look for: they have a fan-shaped silhouette. They have gray, rugged bark, and when the tree is distressed or dying, the bark splits vertically and pulls away from the trunk and the leaves whither, turning ochre as they die. The very earliest signs of a dying elm tree are white speckles on the bark turning to rust, with the fan shaped limbs wilting inward. Wherever you hunt, always check for dying elm trees. If you live in one of the

The fan shape of an elm tree.

locations mentioned above, scout in the fall. The leaves will fall early, and you'll notice stress on the dying elm trees. These are the trees to hunt in the spring; they will have morels growing under their branches.

Once we shared a spot with a close friend, who broke the cardinal rule and told a friend of hers. The third party hunted our spot and came across a very old, very large elm tree that was dying. They found so many morels and, feeling guilty, called our friend to join in the hunt. They couldn't pick all of them before it got dark, so our friend, also feeling guilty, called and told us to pick them. The next morning we went to find the tree. It was a classic scenario. In three days we picked well over four hundred morels under the limbs of that very old elm. The next year we found around fifty morels. We no longer hunt that area because too many people have heard about it, but the last time I checked the tree, all the big limbs had broken off and the trunk was all but fallen over. Classic! As described, a tree will have a large fruiting of morels the first year that it is dying, followed by a year with half as many morels, and even fewer, if any, the third year. If you share a spot, your friend will tell someone, that person will tell someone, and before you know it, too many people know.

White Bark Trees
Birch, Poplar, and Aspen Trees
Birch, poplar, and aspen trees have a great deal in common, including their relationships with morels. Poplar trees are more common in northern states, whereas birch trees can be found throughout the United States. Aspen trees are more common in the western states and at high elevations. They all have shallow root systems and grow in the hills as well as damp areas and along the water's edge. Their bark is white, gray, or peach colored and often peels away from the trunk horizontally. They all have small, round leaves that flicker in the least breeze. It's helpful to check out all the different types in a tree identification book. Northern gray poplars look like they have bands with eyeballs running around the trunks. River birch have peach-colored bark and are common along rivers into the central states, whereas paper birch bark is bright white with horizontal banding tipped in black. It often grows in large stands in the northern states and Canada. Look near aspen trees for morels in mountain regions.

We have occasionally had the privilege to hunt some private land in northern Missouri, twice in the prime season. Beautiful river birch trees grow along the creek that runs through the mid-

Poplars and pines.

dle of the property. The pale coral-colored bark stands out against the green and blue background. These trees deposit a lot of organic material—bark, leaves, and sticks—that needs to decompose. We have found some of the most exquisite gray morels under and near these trees, even when some of them do not appear to be dying. It's possible that flooding or all the debris may encourage the morels to fruit.

In Michigan we hunt an area of the Pigeon River Forest full of white paper birch and poplars, or "popals" as the locals call them. Throughout the area morels grow at the bases of these small trees that are not leafing out. Usually only one or two morels come up at the base of each tree, but there are so many of these trees we always find plenty. In that area the morels always grow on the shaded side of the tree, so we follow that pattern every year.

We stopped for a picnic on an island in the middle of Lake of the Woods on the border between Minnesota and Canada. We watched the eagles fly over, admired the cobalt blue waters, and breathed the perfectly cool, fresh air. Stands of birch and poplar trees as well as pine trees broke up the rocks. We asked our hosts if we could nose around a bit before our shore lunch was ready. In a very short distance we were picking morels and gathering sheets of paper birch bark. Our hosts were surprised to see morels in such a remote location and in such cool conditions. They had hunted morels on the mainland but had never thought to look on the islands. It had been warm (in the sixties) recently, but by the time we got there the daily temperatures had dropped back to the mid to high forties. The morels that came up in the warmer temperatures continued to grow, warmed by the rock and protected by the leaf litter and tree debris.

When we burn hunt out west in the mountains we look for burn areas with aspen trees mixed in with the pines or on the edges of the burns where these trees grow. Blackened burn areas heat up quickly, and the hardwoods of aspen do not burn up like the pine trees, creating shade to hold the ground temperatures. Many morels fruit under these trees. In an area where all the standing trees are blackened with soot, the white bark of the aspens stands out in great contrast. Not only is it beautiful, it makes locating morels easy.

These three tree types—poplar, birch, and aspen—are more commonly associated with black morels or conicas in the burns, but as the season progresses they host gray and yellow morels too.

Cottonwood and Sycamore trees

Hunting beside a river for morels almost always means looking for morels under cottonwood trees. Cottonwood trees are similar to birch in that the leaves are similarly round and flicker in the breeze, and they have gray bark at the base of the trunk with mostly white bark further up the tree trunk. They drop lots of leaves, sticks, and bark throughout the year. In early fall the leaves turn yellow before they fall. However, cottonwood trees reach heights of eighty to one hundred feet, much larger than birch trees, maturing in just twenty years. They have a cottonlike material with their seedpod and are found abundantly along rivers but also in farm fields and wet low-lands. When one of these giants dies, you can expect to find a large batch of morels nearby. We hunted with a group along the Mississippi River, and several guys in the group found a very large, dying cottonwood tree. They picked eighty-five six-inch yellow morels in that one spot. Along the Kansas River cottonwood trees are being logged for pallets. Two years after the logging, morels are being gathered by the pickup truckload. Along the banks of the Platte and Missouri rivers in Nebraska and Iowa, cottonwoods are abundant . . . and so are morels.

The equally large but broader sycamore tree often grows by rivers but also can be found in the hills and in cities. The sycamore has beautiful white bark with patches of tan. It has some of the largest leaves of all trees. The leaves turn lime green, then yellow, and then ochre in early fall. Sycamores are part of the *Acer* genus, or maple family. The leaves smell like maple syrup, and when you dry mushrooms that were picked under maple or sycamore trees, the dried mushrooms smell like maple syrup.

Sycamore trees drop large seedpods and sticks throughout the year. We have a friend in Kansas City who takes his leaf blower to his favorite sycamore tree hunting area to remove the leaves without disturbing the morels. Some of the largest and most unusual morels we ever found were growing under the fallen bark of a huge dying sycamore. The mushrooms were the size of coffee mugs, round, yellow, and somewhat dry with walls half an inch thick. We attributed their girth from growing up through the very dense bark. Sycamore trees are easy to spot at great distances because of their massive size and their striking white bark tipped with black. In the winter when most trees have lost their leaves, these trees can be spotted from great distances.

Messy Trees

Many trees are messy—they lose bark, drop large seedpods or fruit, and drop sticks or small branches. These trees have the potential for producing morels because all the debris must decompose. We've included the cottonwood, and sycamore trees among the white bark trees, but they overlap into the messy tree types because of all the tree debris they produce. Fruit trees make up most of the rest of this category. Although trees that produce nuts and acorns fit this profile, they are not the most likely places to find morels. There may be many reasons for this such as their symbiotic relationship with other types of mushrooms, or that their dense hardwood and deep root system may not be a food source for morels. Since morels are not generally found among trees that produce nuts and acorns, you can better spend your time hunting mushrooms in other places where you'll be more likely to find them.

Hawthorn Trees

Hawthorn trees, sometimes called Jesus trees because of their thorns, thrive in our area. They are very messy trees and morels will fruit near them when they die. We were mushroom hunting on public ground at a nearby lake one spring when we discovered a sizeable batch of twenty or so three-inch tall morels directly under a freestanding, dying hawthorn tree. Many hunters do not think to look under hawthorns, but we have seen this several times.

Fruit Trees and Orchards

Fruit trees are very messy. Birds frequently visit fruit trees for food. Not only do they eat the fruit, but they knock a lot of the fruit to the ground. The birds' attempts at getting fruit off the tree can also cause branches to break and leaves to fall. Fruit trees that are cared for, such as those grown in orchards, are constantly being pruned, which leaves matching root material to decompose. Fallen fruit can provide plenty of food for morels. The rotting fruit returns the sugars or carbohydrates to the soil, which is beneficial for morels. In old or abandoned orchards, not only are the trees messy, but the old trees die.

In Michigan, especially in the Taverse City area (the cherry capital), mushroom hunters target old or abandoned orchards. Not only are the mushroom hunters taking advantage of the messy tree type, but the old (dying) trees provide an easy way to look for morels. We picked a couple pounds of morels in a berry patch one spring, and there weren't any trees nearby. The messy fruit and broken woody briers were as fertile morel hunting grounds as any orchard.

Wild persimmon trees are abundant in Missouri, and you can find morels near them.

Our friend in Michigan has fruit trees in her back yard. She picks morels under them every year.

Maple Trees

In general maple trees have gray, gnarly bark, are fairly tall, and have round to column-shaped upper braches. The leaves are vivid green in the spring and typically form earlier than other tree leaves. They are shaped like a spread out hand and have pointy tips. The Canadian flag has a maple leaf. In the fall the leaves turn anywhere from bright yellow to iridescent orange to brick red. Visit nurseries in the fall to familiarize yourself with the variations of maple trees.

We have a friend in Iowa who checks every maple tree, dead or alive, along the banks of the rivers he hunts. He swears it's the best way to find morels. He shared one of his favorite public places with us, and sure enough, we came across a maple tree that had over eighty big morels in the grass under its branches.

We also found abundant morels in a small area of Illinois where maple trees had been randomly planted. The morels were scattered throughout the five- to seven-inch diameter trees. In tight growing conditions where there is competition for food, water, and sunlight, some trees will dominate and survive, while others will die. Just look for the trees not getting their leaves on when the other trees arc leafing. Look for maple trees or any type of tree growing under close conditions, and find the ones that are dying—that's where the morels will be.

Tulip and Ginko Trees

Tulip and ginkgo trees are usually ornamental trees, and are native to the eastern states. Both tulip and ginkgo trees get quite large, and their leaves have distinctive shapes. Tulip trees have leaves that are broad with four points and have large tulip-shaped greenish flowers in early summer. The ginkgo leaf shape resembles a fan and turns bright yellow in the fall.

We heard from a man in West Virginia, who told of a tulip tree dying in his hometown. He was an avid morel hunter and knew just what to do. Listening to him weave his story was like hearing from someone who just discovered a gold deposit. He said that for two years he found morels by the tree.

Woody Shrubs and Plants

The first time we found black morels in the Kansas City area, they were tucked in under large shrubs. Winter wasn't letting go, and spring temperatures were slow to arrive. Typically you find black morels in open areas of the woods, but these woods didn't have any open areas. We found another batch of morels under a line of bushes at the edge of a field. Most surprising though were the morels we found under blackberry briers. In all three locations the bushes were not near trees.

Bamboo patches and spots where snake grass grows along rivers are often overlooked. We've found eight- to ten-inch morels nestled in the thickets of these woody plants. Because the bamboo and snake grass grow so close together, the morels stay shaded and can grow undetected until quite large. It may not be easy to hunt for morels in these conditions, but it is well worth the effort.

A woman in Michigan described one of her favorite spots as a marshland—no trees, all snake grass. Snake grass is a bright green,

Morels in snake grass.

tubular grass with overlapping joints and dark tips that resemble a snake's head. Be sure to wear clothes you don't care about when hunting in snake grass. When the blades break, fluid comes out and will stain fabric.

In both Illinois and Michigan we found morels nestled into patches of decayed fern before the new spring growth appeared. The morels were nude-colored and extremely hard to see. They seemed extremely fresh, like early black morels, which darken on the edges as they mature. They were a challenge to see, but we kept following the pattern and found more.

Not all morels grow near trees. Debris and decaying root material, whether from a tree, shrub, or grass, provide a food source for morels.

Multiple-Trunk Trees

All trees with multiple trunks are at risk of losing one or more trunks as they age. Water that settles into the trunk crotch eventually drowns one or more of the trunks. We have seen this with ash, birch, and silver maple trees, as well as northern triple-trunk cherry trees and oak trees. You can find this category of trees easily in the woods, and they are worth examining up close. As with other trees, when they die, the root mass becomes food for the morels. These giant trees have very large root systems, which provide a lot of food for the morels, and potentially a lot of morels for you to pick. Oak trees are unlikely to fruit morels but likely will have a fall mushroom called the hen-of-the-woods, a very choice edible mushroom.

Ash Trees

Ash trees have heavily grooved bark that is medium gray with a

Look for dying trees without their leaves.

vertical diamond-shaped pattern. Its leaves mature late in the spring after most other trees already have leaves. In recent years, ash trees have become the dominant tree associated with morels in the Midwest. The emerald ash borer, first discovered in Pennsylvania and moving west and south, has been destroying these magnificent trees and threatens the entire ash tree population of North America. The borer was introduced to the United States through untreated wood brought from its native home in Asia. Borers are transported across the United States in firewood. Some signs of this woodboring pest are crown die-off, small side shoots at the base of an ash tree, D-shaped exit holes in the bark, bark splitting, and

S-shaped tunneling on the trunk inside the bark. The outer bark falls off, and from a distance the tree bark has patches of lighter colored areas. The larvae of the ash borer are similar in size and color to inchworms and have branch-like joints along their bodies.

During the first years of infestation in Michigan we found lots of morels around ash trees. Some of the trees did not have obvious signs of dying, but the bark pattern is so distinctive we checked every ash tree that year. We were excited to go back the next season but learned that the state of Michigan cut down 20,000 infected ash trees in the area. Other states have not responded so dramatically, but that may change.

Ash borer damage.

We showed an ash specimen to some friends who hunted land in south-central Iowa with their cousin who was an elm tree hunter. They were getting discouraged because they weren't finding morels under the usual elm trees, until one of them remembered what we had said about ash trees. They started checking ash trees and ended up spending the rest of the day picking morels.

In an area where a specific type of tree is the target of disease or invasion, morels will respond to those trees more than to others. Maybe the underground organisms communicate so well with the environment that they go where they are needed. So much is yet to be learned about the connection between trees and mushrooms.

We hope that the ash borer invasion makes morels as abundant as they were when Dutch elm disease spread and that this time mushroom hunters use mesh collection bags to spread the spore to grow morels for future generations.

Evergreen Trees

Most forest fires are in evergreen forests. Areas with pine trees and aspens are great for hunting morels. When we hunt places that had forest fires the previous summers, the pattern we chase is different than that of normal spring mushroom hunting in the Midwest. First, we locate the big fires from the previous summer. Then we locate where the professional pickers and buyers will be. And finally we camp in the area of the burns so we aren't spending time traveling back and forth. Once we select the area, we look for the edges of the fires where the trees may be scorched but still have some needles on and where there are aspen trees. Since morels are temperature triggered, you need to find places where trees shade the blackened earth. We have picked black, gray, and yellow morels within inches of each other according to where the sun struck the soil, where the shade was, and where the trunk of a burned down tree blocked the sun and kept the ground cool. The black morel was in the burned out base of the tree stump, the gray morel was in the shade of the stump, and the warmer-temperature yellow morel was out in the open. In forest fire areas morels tend to favor the Douglas fir evergreen tree over other varieties of evergreens.

In southern Iowa, we find morels in an evergreen stand surrounded by a mix of deciduous trees. The needle base under these trees is thick, like fallen leaves. We love this area because the hunting is easy. The morels stick up through the pine needles; the contrasting color makes them easy to see. The pine trees shade the area well, and the morels are usually over five inches tall. We have found both gray and early yellow morels there.

Evergreen boughs keep the ground temperature warm in cool weather and keep the ground cool in warm weather. The right temperature and protective shade allows the morels to grow and spread more spore. In Kentucky and Tennessee, for example, cedar trees are abundant; they hold moisture and the boughs protect the morels. Most people do not think to look under evergreen trees, but the morels are there, hiding.

Oak Trees

Morels generally do not grow near nut- and acorn-producing trees. However, in the Ozarks, where oak trees dominate the landscape, gray morels grow under white oaks. In more natural morel-fruiting woods the morels come up under loose piles of recently fallen oak leaves when a nearby tree is dying, similar to why evergreen trees often have morels fruiting beneath the boughs. The freshly fallen leaves are not yet packed down from winter rains and snows, and morels can grow there protected by the shade. Even in forests where oak trees dominate, you can find morels if you spend your time wisely, searching the most likely places.

Trees to Avoid

We have never found morels near beech, ironwood (hornbeam), locust, or Osage orange, or hedgerow trees. We have never found fruitings of morels under Catalpa trees either, despite their messy seed pods and huge leaves. If you find yourself in areas dominated by any of these varieties of trees, move on. Spend your time hunting morels by the trees likely to host them.

CHAPTER 9

Hunting Morels in the Burns

Hunting the burns is an incredible experience, one that can stretch the season through summer. It is not a hunt for the weekend walker, though. It is very hard work, exceptionally dirty, and most accommodations near burn sites are primitive camping. But there are a lot of great mushrooms to pick.

To locate an area to hunt burns start researching the fall forest fires of the previous year. Look for the long, deep-burning forest fires that cover large amounts of acreage. By springtime information will be available with notices of permit requirements. That's when you know the morels will be there. In Montana the Hungry Horse Ranger Station covers most of that corner of the state's forestry. Usually some portion of the forestry within the ranger station's territory has had burns. When fire information is hard to acquire, call them. Kalispell, Montana, is the nearest city to Hungry Horse with an airport you can fly into, and the nearby towns have hotels and resorts, catering to Glacier National Park traffic. Still, camping takes you closest to the action. We have hunted burns in Alaska, Washington, Idaho, Oregon, Montana, and some areas of Canada.

Whatever burn you hunt, you must first check in with the local ranger station. Call ahead for local requirements; no question is insignificant. Get your permits and fulfill any other requirements such as a film or class on bear behavior. Black bears and grizzly bears both live in many parts of the western United States. Permits

Burn hunting.

for personal use are usually free, but you can only pick a limited number of morels and you must cut them in half from top to bottom when you collect them. Commercial permits allow you to take only the cap of the morel because this is how morels are bought and sold worldwide for commercial use. Generally all mushrooms must be cut, not plucked. For commercial picking the fees vary depending on the state where the fire is located. If you camp in national forestry to pick mushrooms, the fees are higher and you may only stay in specific campgrounds set up for commercial pickers. The fees are higher because it is illegal to profit from this particular type of public land.

You need to be prepared for bears. You must carry out all the food and garbage you have with you. It's good to pack heavy-duty trash bags. If a bear-proof trash receptacle is unavailable you may have to lock the trash in your vehicle. Luckily the bears eat mostly fruits and berries this time of year. The burned areas are void of this type of vegetation, but you still must be aware.

Working an area.

Wear clothes that will protect you and that you don't mind get-ting extremely dirty; you will likely end up throwing them away. Short-sleeved shirts are tempting because the blackened earth heats up during the day; however, what is left of the branches after a burn can be very sharp. For better protection wear long sleeves and pants. Wear good, well-fitting hiking boots with hiking socks, and take along a spare pair of boots. Wear a brimmed hat to protect your head and eyes. Most of the burned areas are on steep slopes; you have to climb over charcoaled fallen trees and slide through crusted-over mud. At the end of each day you will be covered in soot.

The ranger station instructs you to cut the morels from the ground for the future of the mushrooms. We know better! Use either slotted baskets or mesh bags to keep your mushrooms fresh, even in the burns where you pick all sizes and types. Unlike most areas where you want to release spore through the mesh bag for future generations of morels, a burn site has an abundance of morels due to the trauma of the burn and the available food source. Morels will continue to grow there in the future, but not in the same quantities as they do following a forest fire. Like pruning, cutting the morels gently from the mycelia (similar to a root) will encourage new morels to grow from that same rootlike (mycelia) source days later. We hunted a burn area and picked hundreds of gray morels. Just a few days later we returned. Hunting in our own footsteps and within inches of our cut-off stems we found fresh morels. In fact, areas with cut stems produced more morels than areas we hunted that showed no evidence of previous pickers. Similar to pruning, cutting morels stimulated new growth during the current year.

Packing out morels. Each box holds approximately six to eight pounds.

When we hunt the Montana burn sites, we are in awe of nature's ability to rebound. Areas that were black and barren just a few days earlier become speckled with bright green vegetation and fruited with fungi. As snowpack and glaciers melt, clear water runs down the mountains. In addition to morels, we picked chanterelles, oyster mushrooms, boletuses, and corals. We saw several inedible species; especially beautiful were the bright orange tiny cup fungi that covered large areas at once.

This is an incredible experience for any avid morel hunter with the courage to get dirty, be uncomfortable, and hike strenuously through downed timber while climbing a mountainside. The rewards are views of awesome scenery juxtaposed with blackened

Lots of burn morels.

soil and burnt trees, dotted with the bounty of some of the most beautiful morels you will ever pick.

We have hunted burns in the Northwest territory. We hunted in snow, got stuck thigh-high in mud pits, nearly slid off the side of one mountain, and spotted eagles, moose, and bear. We shared mountainsides with gun-carrying hunters, were stopped many times to have our permits checked, and were spied on by buyers. This is really hard work. We don't ever remember being so tired . . . or so satisfied.

PART II

Preserving Morels

Preserving morels may be the most challenging part of the sport for many, but it need not be. Many people are tempted to put fresh morels into salted water to remove the bugs and dirt, as you would soak wild game, but mushrooms should not be soaked. They won't get dirty if you cut them, and carrying them in a mesh bag allows most of the bugs to leave naturally.

What follows are tried-and-true methods of enjoying morels and preserving them from the hunt to the table.

CHAPTER 10

Preserving Morels to Eat Fresh

Morels stay fresh for about two weeks if you collect them and refrigerate them appropriately. The first part of the process is picking the morels correctly: always cut the morel at the base of the stem without getting dirt on the mushroom. Morels come out of the ground clean. If you don't get them dirty when you pick them, you won't have to contend with it later. Next, gently place them in a mesh collection bag. Mesh bags are the best method of carrying morels to allow the spore to release back into the environment for reproduction, and the mesh bag allows the morels to breathe, keeping them fresh. Think about putting a banana in a plastic bag and carrying it around all day in the woods. It would bruise and sweat and likely turn to mush. The same is true for morels.

Make sure you bring a cooler to transport your morels. The best way to keep your morels cool and dry is to put sealed bags of ice in the bottom of the cooler with a piece of cardboard on top of the ice cut about one inch smaller than the bottom of the cooler. That will let the cool air circulate without causing condensation on the morels. Keep the lid cracked open: this too will keep condensation at bay. Do not put the cooler in the trunk of your car. When it's hot out keep the cooler on the shaded side of the car and run the air conditioner. If it's cool out and you need the heater, make sure the cooler is on the backseat out of the draft. Keep the morels cool and dry.

Keep morels cool and dry.

When you get home, follow the instructions below for preserving the morels. Do not wash them or immerse them in water until you are ready to cook them.

CLEANING AND SOAKING
For Immediate Use
If you want to eat your morels right away, gently roll them out of the bag into a colander. Use your sink hose to spray the mushrooms, freeing them of dirt and bugs. If the mushrooms have begun to dry, soak them in a glass bowl filled with water only long enough to get out your pans and ingredients for cooking the morels. When everything is ready to cook pour off the water, rinse them again, and pat them dry with a paper towel or tea towel.

For Later That Day or the Next Day
To prepare the mushrooms to eat later in the day or the next day, line a glass bowl with a towel, and then place the mushrooms in the bowl with paper towels between layers. Place a paper towel on top of the morels with a damp paper towel on top of it. The top towel

Morels keep for several days in a paper sack in the refrigerator.

will keep the morels fresh without any direct moisture, which can spoil them. The layered towels keep the rest of the morels from spoiling if one goes bad. You can't see mold on the interior of the morel and if you see mold on the surface of a morel cut it off or throw away that mushroom. When you are ready to cook them, only clean the morels you are going to cook. After a few days in the refrigerator, the morels may be a bit dried out. It may take twenty minutes of soaking for them to plump up. The mushrooms will have the same texture and flavor and be as firm as they were when they were picked.

If you are going to cook the morels later that day, you can put the mesh bag of mushrooms into a paper grocery sack and store it in the refrigerator or in a prepared cooler. Cardboard boxes also work well. Cut the sides of the boxes so they are three inches tall for one layer of morels. Stack the boxes full of morels at angles so the box sides keep the pressure off the morels. For small batches, you can transfer the morels into a paper lunch sack, roll the top down, and store it in the refrigerator. Any bugs will go into hibernation like they do on a cold night in the woods. When you are ready to cook the morels, follow the directions above for cleaning and soaking.

For Up to Two Weeks

Keeping morels for up to two weeks takes more preparation. First, sort morel mushrooms by freshness. The whitest stems are the freshest; stems yellow as they age. Place a towel in the bowl, and place the morels in the bowl with layers of paper towels in between. Place the freshest and firmest morels at the bottom of a glass bowl, and the oldest (ones with yellowish to golden stems and any signs of deterioration on the cap) on top. Place a paper towel on top of the mushrooms with a damp paper towel on top of that. Don't worry about bugs. As you were walking in the woods and the morels were drying, many of the bugs left. When you put the bowl of mushrooms in the refrigerator, any remaining bugs will go into hibernation.

To keep prime specimens really nice for up to two weeks wrap each one individually in toilet paper. Place them in a bowl or box. Check on them every day until you are ready to cook them. The paper may stick to the mushroom but will release when you put them in water to clean them.

Be sure to keep the morels in the warmer part of the refrigerator like the vegetable bin; otherwise they will freeze like radishes and become inedible. We keep a separate refrigerator in the garage set at a warmer setting just for morels. In our kitchen refrigerator

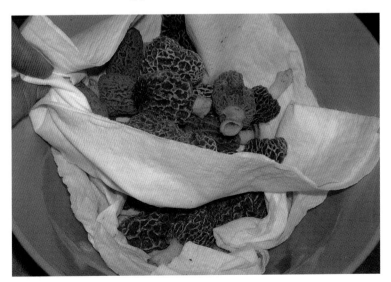

Layer morels between paper towels.

we place a hand towel around the outside of the bowl to keep it warmer.

Every day, mist or sprinkle water on the damp paper towel on top. This will provide enough moisture to keep the morels fresh without causing them to spoil. They will dry out some in the refrigerator, so before you cook them, clean them as described, and then place them in another glass bowl with water. Since they aren't totally dry, they will quickly regain the moisture content they had when picked. Allow twenty to thirty minutes of soaking for every two days in the refrigerator beyond the first day. Finally, give them a good rinse to release the rest of the dirt and bugs, keeping the mushrooms submerged under the running water. Pat them dry and cook.

The paper towels will have yellow to golden colored spore on them, which you can take back to the woods. Save the yellowed paper towels in a paper sack, and next time you go to woods where morels can grow, tear the paper towels into pieces and bury them under the leaves.

In summary, pick morels carefully to keep them clean, collect them in a mesh bag, keep them dry, store them in a glass bowl with paper towels between the layers, and reconstitute them in water and rinse them just before cooking.

PRESERVING A SPECIMEN MOREL

Photographs are great, but some mushroom hunters want more than a picture. Having a morel professionally freeze-dried can be costly, so the following are two other ways to keep your special find.

The floral departments of craft stores often have a liquid mix that turns solid that makes flowers look as though they are standing in water. To use this for a morel, you need a clear container that is only slightly larger than the morel. Pour half an inch of the liquid into the bottom of the container, stand the morel in the center of the liquid, and continue filling the container until the morel is completely covered. Dry following the package recommendations.

The second method for preserving a morel takes more effort and some refrigerator space. Use a caulking gun to fill the inside of the morel with white or clear silicone. Fill it to capacity but do not overfill it or the morel will split. Carefully place the morel in a box with cushioning to help it retain its original shape. Place it in the warmest part of the refrigerator and let it slowly dry out. Rotate the morel every few days or if you notice it becoming flat on one side. It may take a few weeks to fully dry out. When it is completely dry, you may have to trim the silicone bottom so the morel can stand. You can then stand it on a wooden base with a glass dome over it. If you want to mount it to a board, consider imbedding a screw in the silicone after it has dried slightly.

CHAPTER 11

Preserving Morels for Storage

The morel mushroom season is short. In the spring all we want to do is hunt and eat morels. To enjoy eating morels throughout the rest of the year, dry some. Internationally all mushrooms are sold fresh, dried, or canned. Canning is hard work, and the canned morels cannot be cooked like fresh morels. The drying method is easy, inexpensive, gets rid of all the bugs naturally, and takes very little hands-on preparation. Dried morels will keep indefinitely (for long-term storage use glass jars). Best of all, the reconstituted morels can be cooked as if you picked them today. Dry the best produce, as the mushrooms will only be as good reconstituted as they were before drying.

Straight from the woods, separate (cut) caps from stems and then spread the mushrooms out on a nonmetallic screen outdoors for eight hours to allow air to circulate around them. Do not wash or rinse the morels before drying. They will be light as paper and hard as rocks when they are fully dry. The first time you do it, you'll think the morels are ruined because they shrink and look so funny. Morels are over ninety percent water, and drying them removes all the water. It's that easy.

The texture of the caps and stems are entirely different—they don't dry the same, and they don't reconstitute the same. Depending on the amount of morels we're drying, we usually eat the stems right away. When we dry the stems, we store them separately. You can grind them to use as a seasoning, but remember, they are not clean. Reconstitute them and clean them before cooking, or dry clean them (use a mushroom brush to knock off any dirt) and use them in a recipe that has a high moisture content and will reach a rolling boil to reconstitute them properly. One pound of morels dries to two ounces; two ounces of dried morels reconstitutes to one pound (an 8 to 1 ratio). This will come in handy when you cook with dried morels.

SCREEN METHOD

A screen for drying morels can be as simple as a mesh fabric strung between trees or a box with window screening attached to it. We use a portable screen made from a five-foot length of black, non-metallic window screen material with two 36-inch-long dowels stapled to each end. You can roll it up and take it anywhere you hunt morels. If you start the drying process where you hunt, the bugs leave naturally after just a few hours of drying and as the mushrooms dry spore is released into the area where it has the best chance to make more mushrooms. Stretch the screen over logs, coolers, picnic table benches, or anywhere else where there is at least a foot of air space below the screen. This will allow air to circulate around the morels and help the morels to dry out quickly. Black mesh also speeds up the drying process. Aluminum frame, nonmetallic window screens work well, too. Most replacement window screen fabric at hardware stores is thirty-six inches wide. Buy either fiberglass or nylon mesh in whatever length you need.

Boxed wooden frames can be stacked, leaving room for ventilation. The frames can be made to fit any situation. Additionally, morels drying on these screens can be sorted and spread out on the screens at a campsite and then taken to the woods while you hunt. In this way you can not only safeguard your morels, but also release the spore back into its own environment where it can do the most good.

These are 4-by-8 screens for drying morels.

When we get in after dark from mushroom hunting and want to dry a portion of our catch, we leave the morels in their mesh bags and hang them in the garage or basement in a cool, dry place until morning. Remember, the coolest, driest place is best. The next day we put the screens covered in mushrooms out on our deck and let nature do the rest. By the time we come in from another all-day hunt, we can start the process all over.

On windy days, stack a second screen frame over the screen frame holding the mushrooms or cover the screen with cheesecloth and tuck the edges under the frame to secure it. As the mushrooms dry out and become as light as paper they can blow off the screen.

MESH BAG METHOD

We are chasers. We hunt morels all over the country. We have to be able to adapt to a variety of circumstances. Once, in central Iowa, we collected morels at a state park and dried them at our picnic site. We strung large mesh laundry bags from trees with bungee cords. On the way home, we hung them in the back of our van over a layer of newspaper.

Morel spore is sticky and can be difficult to clean from the interior of your vehicle, so cover any areas where the spore will collect with newspaper. You can take the newspaper out to the woods and spread pieces of it under leaves, returning the spore to the wild.

We often stay in hotel rooms while on the road hunting and teaching people how to hunt morels. The limited space and time constraints make drying morels a challenge. We have found that morels will dry out in their mesh bags if you spread them in a thin layer in the bag and hang it on the back of a chair near the register. On a cool night, turn the heater on low and let the fan run. If it's hot, turn the air conditioner on low and let the fan blow. Remember, keep the morels cool and dry with air circulating around them. They can finish drying on the dashboard of your car. Again, leave them in their mesh bags, but spread them out. The black mesh will attract the sun, and the mushrooms will become hard as rocks and light as air. When they don't give, the morels are ready to put away.

REFRIGERATOR METHOD

If you are in a humid part of the country, you can use your refrigerator to dry morels. Most modern refrigerators are frost-free, meaning the moisture in the foods kept in them tends to evaporate.

Place the morels on paper plates or spread them out in shallow cardboard boxes. Be sure they are not touching each other. It helps if you have a second refrigerator, because this method requires a lot of space. Leave them in the refrigerator for up to two weeks, checking them occasionally. If one starts to mold, cut off that part of the mushroom or remove the entire mushroom. Make sure the morels are completely dry before storing them. For the first few weeks, store them in small batches in paper lunch sacks or spread them out on a screen in a cool, dry place. Morels cannot be over-dried. Make sure they are hard as rocks and light as paper before storing them. Dried morels will not give when you squeeze them. Just one morel with moisture can spoil an entire batch.

As a last resort, you can finish drying morels in an oven warming bin at the lowest possible temperature, leaving the door open. Avoid heat whenever possible, though, because the morels will harden into little black rocks and they will not reconstitute. Remember, cool and dry is best, and do not wash or rinse morels before drying them. Morels that get wet will dry black and hard, never to return to their natural condition. Reconstitute morels and then clean them just before you cook them (more about this later). Do not seal them in glass until you are positive they are dry. Any condensation can ruin the entire batch.

DEHYDRATORS

Dehydrators are great for finishing the drying process, but we do not recommend starting the drying process there. Residential dehydrators are small and usually do not have enough airflow and ventilation, and they use heat in the drying process, which makes the reconstituted morels chewy. The reason to dry morels is to make the most of a good season and to store the surplus for future meals. All the other drying methods require little work, freeing you up to spend more time hunting. To use a dehydrator, you need to cut up your mushrooms into small enough pieces to fit in the small space, trade out batches as they dry, and stay with the unit until all the morels are dry. The final reason we don't use dehydrators is that during the drying process spore is expelled from the morels and can clog the machine. Worse yet, it stays on the morels and in the machine rather than returning to nature. The machine will be difficult to clean because the sticky spores get baked on the surface, and the dried-on spore dust cannot be cleaned from the morels. Where do the bugs go? Like the spore they become trapped in the machine and on the morels.

Floor model dehydrators work better. Most are roomy, designed primarily for making jerky. These are best for finish-

Finish drying in a dehydrator.

ing the drying process. As with other drying methods, separate the morel caps from the stems. Spread them out on the racks so the mushrooms do not touch. Set the temperature at 140 degrees for eight to ten hours depending on when you can get back to it. Do not allow the dehydrator to turn off when you aren't there. Humidity can return quickly, ruining your mushrooms.

It's best to start the drying process outdoors for at least two hours, ideally near the woods so that the bugs and spore can return to nature.

STORING AND RECONSTITUTING DRIED MORELS

Store dried morels in a cool, dry place in a brown paper bag for short-term storage. For long-term storage, transfer the morels to glass jars, only after you are certain they are dry.

Store dried morels in glass jars.

To reconstitute them for cooking, measure out the amount of morels you want to cook. One ounce of dried morels (approximately one cup) reconstitutes to eight ounces. If a recipe calls for a pound of morels, reconstitute two ounces. Measure morels by weight rather than by volume.

To reconstitute morels, place them in a glass bowl. Pour in six cups of cool to room temperature water for each ounce of morels. Use a small plate to submerge the mushrooms under the water, and put the bowl in a cool place. To be fully reconstituted the morels must soak for at least four hours. Do not leave them in water longer than twelve hours, or they will begin to deteriorate. If you want morels for breakfast, put them in water in the refrigerator just before going to bed. If you want morels for dinner when you come home from work, put them in water before you go to work.

The water will turn a beautiful amber color and will smell and taste just like the morels. To use the water for broth, remove the morels with a slotted spoon. Filter the water through a coffee filter, and bring it to a rolling boil to kill any bacteria. The broth will only keep in the refrigerator for a day or two. You can freeze the boiled broth to use later. The broth is great in soups, over roasts and chicken, in rice and risotto, and so on.

Once the morels are reconstituted, wash them, and let them drain in a colander. Just before cooking, pat the morels dry.

There is nothing better than a fresh morel, but reconstituted morels are very close in texture and flavor. They cook more quickly and taste a little stronger than fresh morels, but they still taste great. The dried black morels really seem to intensify in flavor; we liken it to the difference between fresh apricots and the stronger flavor of the dried apricot. White morels reconstitute just as well.

FREEZING MORELS

The half-cap morels are higher in moisture content than any other morel variety, so they do not dry well. The best way to keep them is to fry them with bacon until fully cooked, package them in Ziploc bags, and store them in the freezer. Date them and use them by the end of the year they were harvested.

Freezing Morels for Short-term Use

Many people freeze morels. Keep in mind, though, that this is a short-term storage method, for storing them no more than three to six months, as bacteria can continue to grow in the freezer. The mushrooms need to stay completely frozen, so be aware of power outages, especially in the Midwest. Hollow morels thaw relatively quickly, allowing bacteria to develop, and refreezing makes them mushy.

The basic freezer method is to batter the morels in your favorite batter recipe, then partially cook them, and then put them on a cookie sheet to freeze. When the mushrooms are frozen, slide them into freezer bags, and put them back into the freezer. When you're ready to cook the morels, take them out of the freezer and carefully put them directly into hot oil to cook. Frost-free freezers can separate some of the moisture in the morel before it freezes solid. There may be spattering when you put them in oil.

Another freezing method is to put morels straight from the woods on cookie sheets, freeze them, and then move them into freezer bags. Others freeze morels in water. All of these methods are labor intensive and take up valuable freezer space, and the mushrooms should be eaten within a few months.

There are other methods to preserve morels, such as canning, but they take a lot of time and hard work. Drying is the best method; remember, do not get them wet, and keep them cool and dry to preserve them.

HOW TO PRESERVE MORELS WHILE TRAVELING

If you travel to hunt for morels, the biggest obstacle is how to keep your mushrooms fresh until you get home.

Once mushrooms are picked, heat and humidity are the enemies, and while you are traveling, you may not be in an area long enough to fully sun-dry the morels. Instead, use a combination of the refrigerator storage method and sun drying. To begin, decide how many morels you want to keep fresh for eating right away and how many to dry for later use. Remember to choose the best specimens to dry, as morels will only reconstitute to be as good as they were fresh. Cook and eat right away any broken pieces and those that appear to be older (those that have yellowing stems and frayed edges on the cap ridges) because they won't keep as well.

For the morels you want to keep fresh, bring along an extra cooler. Put ice in a sealed plastic bag in the bottom of the cooler. Next, put in a couple of layers of newspaper or cardboard cut an inch smaller than the inside of the cooler; this keeps the fresh morels away from the moisture from the ice. Leave the mushrooms in the mesh collection bag. Keep the lid cracked open on the cooler to prevent condensation from collecting on the morels. Keep the cooler out of the sun and in the cool part of the car. If you are comfortable with the air conditioning on, the morels will be too. If you need to put on the car's heater, put the morels on the back seat away from the heat vents. Follow the directions in chapter 10 for keeping your mushrooms fresh once you get them home.

For the morels you want to dry, there are a couple of ways to transport them. Our favorite method is to keep them in their mesh collection bags, and spread them out in a thin layer on the dashboard. The black mesh fabric will draw the heat of the sun, and the morels will begin to dry out. Running the dashboard fan vents helps too. Use warm air if it's chilly out and air conditioning if it's hot. Be aware that expelling spore can be strong smelling and can cause congestion for people with allergies. When you get home with your morels follow the directions for completing the drying process from earlier in this chapter.

The following drying method is good if you are hunting a few hours or overnight away from home. This method takes more planning. You'll need several large mesh laundry bags, preferably black, enough foam board to fit the bags, and some twine. Use a box cutter to cut the foam to fit inside the bags. Cut rows of rectangle openings in the foam board to hold the morels, stabilizing them as you travel. Slide the modified foam boards into the mesh bags. Pile the completed bags onto each other. Next, cut four 40-inch lengths of twine. Starting with one corner of the bag, tie the twine to the bottom bag. Ten inches up the rope, tie the twine to the next bag in the same corner. Repeat this until all the bags at all the corners are tied. When you hold the tops of the strings the bags will be suspended from each other by the twine. Tie the twine to four spots inside your vehicle, suspending the bags to dry your morels as you travel. You'll need to gauge how much room you have in your vehicle and adjust the system to fit. You can make this drying rack as large or small as space allows. Just make sure you maintain the space between the layers of morels for ventilation, and put a layer of newspaper or plastic under the drying morels so the spore doesn't ruin the interior of your vehicle.

Remember to finish drying the morels before putting them into paper sacks for storage. Once they rattle like rattlesnake tails and become hard as rocks and light as air, they are ready for long-term storage in a cool and dry place. You cannot over-dry a morel, but one that is not completely dry can ruin an entire batch if sealed. Remember, for short-term storage put the dried morels in a brown paper bag. For long-term storage use glass containers.

PART III

Preparing Morels to Eat

Readying morels to cook and eat is an art. We have asked many people how to clean and cook morels, but everyone has different answers and few, if any, are right. Many people put morels in salt water when they get home, which only makes them slimy and salty. Many believe that when the crust of the batter is toasted, the morel inside is cooked too, but that's not necessarily so. Read on to learn the proper ways of cleaning morels and a definitive way to ensure morels are cooked thoroughly. Remember, all mushrooms are hard to digest until they are thoroughly cooked. The basic recipes that follow tell you how to prepare the mushrooms correctly to add into other recipes or to eat as is. This section will teach you how to enjoy eating morels, one of the best reasons to hunt them.

CHAPTER 12

Cleaning Morels

The best method of cleaning morels is not to get them dirty in the first place. Morels come out of the ground clean. When you cut them off at the base of the stem they are clean. If dirt gets in a mesh bag, it will spread into the crevices of the other morels in your bag, making them all dirty and preventing them from expelling spore. Dirt is hard to loosen from the crevices of a morel. The recommended way to clean morels—and all mushrooms—is the dry method: use a soft bristle brush and gently brush away the dirt. Grocery store mushrooms are grown in a sterile substrate; brushing alone may be enough for them. However, morels come from the wild and should be washed just prior to cooking. Using your sink sprayer, loosen any stubborn dirt from the crevices of the mushrooms and then submerge the morels in a water bath. This will release the bugs from the morels and wash away any dirt. Gently transfer the morels into a colander and let them drain. Just before cooking, pat them dry with a towel.

Mushrooms that have survived a rain that splashed dirt onto them are the hardest mushrooms to get clean. The rainwater has already caused damage to the morels, so plan to eat them right away. Take them home and immediately clean them. The best way to do this is to put them in a bowl, hold your hand over the top of the morels, and fill the bowl with cool water, keeping the morels submerged. Then, using the kitchen sink sprayer gently spray the morels until the water runs clear. Cook them immediately.

Aside from removing dirt, you also need to rid the mushrooms of any bugs. Slugs, large bugs, and snails are easy to remove when you pick the morels. Carrying the morels in mesh bags allows the tiny mites to leave as the morels' surfaces dry. To eliminate all the tiny mites, follow the drying method, cutting the morels into ringlets to let the bugs go free. If you don't want to completely dry the morels but want to rid the morels of most of the bugs, set the mushrooms outside to dry for two hours. The mushrooms will then be free of most bugs. To return them to their plump selves, put the morels in water for about half an hour. Since they are only slightly dried, they should come back rather quickly. Squeeze them to check for the texture they had when they were picked. Then they are ready to be cooked.

Another way to rid morels of bugs is to first put them in a paper sack in the refrigerator for a few hours. The bugs will go into a state of hibernation in the cold. When you are ready to cook the morels, submerge them in a bowl of water; continue running the water until there are no more bugs.

CHAPTER 13

Cooking Morels

We have talked to a lot of people about cooking morels, and the most common question is how to tell when the morels are fully cooked. Do not undercook morels, as mushrooms are not easily digestible. Fully cooking them not only brings out the full flavor, but also kills any bacteria in them and makes them more digestible. When sautéing morels, the morels are done when the mushrooms make a popping sound, like bacon when it's crisping. When deep-frying morels with a batter, the morels will float to the top when the batter is done; the morel itself is done when the fried mushroom shakes and then releases bubbles. The bubbles are the indicator.

The first time you eat any wild mushroom, try a small sample. If you don't have a reaction (flulike symptoms) within twenty-four hours, eat on. We eat morels throughout the year, and our bodies are used to them. We usually eat small amounts as condiments or appetizers to our meal. When fresh mushrooms are available, you might be tempted to cook a big batch and eat them all, but it's better to start the season with small batches, like appetizers, working up to larger amounts (like the main meal) toward the end of the season.

Morels, like all mushrooms, cook more evenly when you cut and separate the caps and stems. Caps and stems have different textures and cook differently. Stems take a minute or two longer to

Separate caps and stems for cooking.

cook than caps. Cutting the morels into ringlets allows you to cook the inside and the outside of the morel evenly with full contact with the skillet. When you sauté morels in butter or oil, they first become very soupy as the moisture cooks out of the mushrooms. Further along in the cooking process the moisture diminishes and the morels begin to make a popping sound. If you are using real butter the butter will be clarified at this point.

When you are batter frying morels, it is much harder to hear the popping sound over the oil itself popping, so be sure to allow the morels plenty of time to cook. When the batter is cooked, the morels will float to the top. The fried mushrooms will shake and release bubbles when they are fully cooked.

Most people eat their morels sautéed, fried, or deep-fried. But if you're adding them to a recipe, morels should be precooked. Each of the basic recipes that follow can be varied to suit your family.

BASIC RECIPES

Because of the hunting methods we developed and shared in this book, we have an abundance of dried morels to enjoy year round. Most often we like to savor the flavor of the morel in its basic form. The basic ways to cook morels are sautéed, deep-fried, skillet fried, or cooked with ham or bacon.

You can enjoy morels cooked by themselves, or add them to more complex recipes like risotto, soufflé, or quiche.

Sautéed Morels

Clean the morels, pat them dry, and cut them into ringlets of equal size. Separate the caps from the stems.

Add 2–3 tablespoons of butter and 1–2 tablespoons of extra virgin olive oil to a skillet on medium-high heat. Canola oil, peanut oil, and grape seed oil all work well too. The oil helps keep the butter from burning.

Add a small amount of granulated or chopped fresh garlic. Mushrooms take on the flavors of whatever they are cooked with.

Ringlets.

Go light on the seasonings, and add salt and pepper when the mushrooms come out of the skillet.

Fill the bottom of the pan with morels, starting with the stems and then the caps a minute or two later. Stir gently. Don't crowd the skillet—you may need to cook them in separate batches. The morels will first become soupy, but the liquid will evaporate as they cook. When the butter is clarified and the mushrooms make a popping noise similar to bacon sizzling, they are done. Serve warm with the clarified butter. They are best served with a light cracker and strong cheese like aged New York or Wisconsin cheddar. Match with a semisweet fruity wine.

Use flavored oil, such as sesame oil, to alter the flavor of the morels. A touch of soy sauce gives them a slight Asian saltiness. Use a variety of herbs based on your tastes. Start out with a light touch. Morels absorb the flavors they are cooked with.

One of the joys of finding a lot of morels is preserving them and experimenting with flavors based on the season. Sautéed morels are good over venison and domestic roasts and can be used as the base for cream of morel soup.

Deep-fried Morels

Although we like eating our morels sautéed because it brings out the earthy flavor of the mushroom, many people prefer them fried. The coating adds texture and crunch but it can also overpower the flavor of the morel.

Any deep skillet or electric skillet will work for deep-frying morels. We use a wok with a wire drip rack on the side. Pour enough oil in the pan so that it is deep enough to cover the morel pieces twice. As the oil heats on medium–high heat, dip the morel pieces in beaten egg and dredge them in seasoned flour. When the oil is hot, gently slide the morels into the oil. When the morels are done, set them on the rack for a few minutes and then onto a plate lined with paper towels. Sprinkle with salt and pepper to taste.

You can also use a cracker crumb or breadcrumb mix instead of the seasoned flour. Liquid batter is also excellent, especially for the large morels cut into ringlets. Tempura batter has a much lighter flavor, and beer batter has a few more calories.

Serve fried morels with cheese bites and fresh fruit for a wonderful finger-food dinner.

Skillet-fried Morels

Melt butter in a cast-iron skillet with a small amount of lard to keep the butter from burning. Dredge the morel ringlets in flour, then egg, and then flour again. Carefully lay the morels in pan. When one side is crisp, turn the morels. When they start popping, they are done.

Morels and Bacon

This works with all varieties of morels. When we find a lot of half-cap morels this is what we do with all of them. Render bacon with half-caps to make a sauce for roasts, wild game, rice or pasta dishes, or eggs. For a gourmet grilled cheese sandwich put a few tablespoons of this recipe between the cheese slices.

Use a quarter pound of bacon (or ham) for each pound of morels. Cut the bacon into small pieces. Fry the bacon until crisp. The bacon must be cooked to the desired crispness before you add the morels. Add prepared morels cut into ringlets—first the stems and a minute or so later the caps. If you are using half-cap morels, the stems do not need to be cooked separately from the caps. As it cooks, the liquid will become clear and the morels will make a popping sound. Remove immediately from the heat. Drain off any excess liquid (it can be saved and used to season meat). We prefer to use hickory smoked ham or bacon; the bacon produces a saltier version of the recipe. If you are combining this with another recipe, save the drained liquid and substitute it for part of the liquid or fat of the dish.

MOREL QUICHE

Makes one pie.

1 lb. morels	$^3/_4$ cup Bisquick
$^1/_4$ lb. bacon or ham	3 eggs
$^1/_2$ cup chopped onion	shake of pepper
$^1/_4$ cup chopped green pepper	dash of salt
$^1/_4$ cup chopped red pepper	dash of nutmeg
1$^1/_2$ cup shredded Swiss cheese	

Preheat oven to 400 degrees. Prepare the bacon and morel recipe (or ham variation). Put the mixture in a 10-inch, buttered glass pie dish. Add onions, green and red peppers, and cheese. Mix the Bisquick, eggs, salt, and pepper in a bowl and pour over the ingredients in the pie dish. Bake for 35 minutes or until a toothpick inserted in the quiche comes out clean.

RICE PILAF WITH MORELS

1 lb. morels
$^1/_4$ lb. bacon or 3 T. butter and 1 T. oil
2 cups uncooked long-grain rice
$^1/_3$ cup chopped green onions
3$^1/_2$ cups water
Salt and pepper to taste

Prepare either basic sautéed morels or bacon and morels in a large skillet. When fully cooked, add two cups of uncooked rice. Let it sizzle until most of the rice pops. Add chopped green onions and water. Cover and steam for about twenty minutes, or until the water has been absorbed. Serve with game meat, pheasant, or any kind of roast.

ZUCCHINI AND MOREL CASSEROLE

$^1/_2$ lb. morels	2–3 T. butter
$^2/_3$ cup chopped onion	6 eggs
1 cup sliced zucchini	shake of pepper
$^1/_4$ tsp. basil	$^1/_4$ tsp. oregano
$^1/_2$ cup shredded Colby cheese	dash of salt

Preheat oven to 350 degrees. Butter the bottom and sides of a 9-by-13-inch glass baking dish. Prepare the basic sautéed morel recipe. With a slotted spoon, place the morels in the bottom of the baking dish. Cook the onions in the same pan that you cooked the morels in, using the same butter. When the onions are almost clear, add the zucchini slices. Cook until tender. Using a rubber spatula, scrape the vegetables and remaining butter into the baking dish.

Whisk the eggs with the herbs and spices. Pour over the morels and vegetables. Bake ten minutes or until almost firm.

Spread the top with cheese, place back in the oven, and bake until cheese melts, approximately ten more minutes. Serve as a side dish or cut into squares for an appetizer.

MOREL AND CHEESE OMELET

Prepare either sautéed morels or the bacon and morel recipe.

Scoop the morels out of the pan with a slotted spoon, and set them aside. Whisk three eggs, and pour them into the pan. Cover and cook for two minutes. Take off the lid and fold the morels into the eggs. Sprinkle with your favorite cheese. With a spatula, fold the eggs in half. Cook until eggs are firm and cheese is melted.

MOREL CARBONARA

$^1/_2$ lb. bacon

$1^1/_2$ to 2 lbs. morels

3 cloves of garlic, crushed

1 cup of heavy cream

4 eggs

1 cup grated Parmesan cheese

1 lb. linguine

Prepare the basic bacon and morel recipe. Add three crushed cloves of garlic. Cook the linguine according to the package directions. Beat the eggs and cream together in a medium-sized bowl and pour into the pan when the morels are fully cooked. Stirring constantly, cook just until warm. Remove from heat and add in the cheese. In a large serving bowl, toss the drained linguine with the sauce. Sprinkle with nutmeg and additional cheese. Serve immediately.

MOREL BÉCHAMEL

Reconstitute one ounce of dried morels in four cups of water for four hours. After reconstituting the morels, filter them from the liquid by pouring them through a coffee filter. Reserve the liquid. Rinse and pat the mushrooms dry. Sauté the morels, and then add 2 T. flour. Stir constantly, until the mixture is smooth and begins to brown. Add half of the reserved liquid. Stir until smooth. The gravy will not reach its full thickness until the liquid comes to a boil. If it thickens too fast, add more liquid, up to three cups, depending on the consistency you prefer. Add salt and pepper to taste. Garlic is good, too; mix it in as the gravy thickens. Serve over mashed potatoes with fried chicken, pork chops, or steak.

MARINATED MORELS

6 jelly jars
1$^1/_2$ lbs. small, tightly formed morels
Garlic cloves (1 or 2 per jar)
1 cup olive or canola oil
$^1/_2$ cup vinegar
8 T. water
2 t. granulated garlic
2 t. dried oregano
2 t. dried basil
4 t. dried chopped onions
Salt and pepper (a sprinkle of salt, a shake of pepper)

Mix liquids with the last five ingredients in a measuring cup. Mix well and immediately divide into the jars.

Bring morels to a rapid boil. Boil three minutes, strain, and immediately put into an ice bath to stop the cooking.

Divide them into the jars, approximately a quarter pound each, with a clove or two of garlic. Tighten down the lid, shake well, and then refrigerate. They are good to eat in about two weeks.

You can substitute packaged Italian dressing mix. It may take two jars to cover all the morels.

There are lots of recipes for morels, but these are our family favorites. The best recipe may be the simplest: morels sautéed in butter with garlic, served with crackers and cheese. For more recipes, see *Old Fashioned Mushroom Recipes* (Bear Wallow Publishers). Finding ways to enjoy the flavor of morels is easier than finding morels.

PART IV

Public Access

You have to be creative to find places to hunt mushrooms. This collection of agency phone numbers, websites, and rules and regulations pertaining to the locations will help you find areas in which to hunt. When you chase mushrooms it's especially important to hunt legally and safely on public lands. Mushroom hunting on private land without permission is not only trespassing but also poaching, or stealing. You can be prosecuted for it. Hunting mushrooms on public land where it is not allowed is also poaching. When in doubt, ask. Be an ethical mushroom hunter.

Mushroom regulations mostly fall in the wild plant category, but they are not technically a plant—so don't assume it is okay to pick them. Morels are not plants, nor are they animals; therefore, some places do not have laws specifically governing morels. In these instances, you should check with the local ranger or park officer. (You can also ask if the ranger knows good hunting areas.) In parts of the country where mushroom hunting is more common, many states have specific rules for mushroom hunting. For instance, Missouri State Parks have a daily two-gallon limit for personal consumption.

One caution about using the Internet to research: Don't believe everything you read. Some sites legitimately track mushroom sightings, while others, especially blogs and forums, contain questionable information. The best hunters hunt in the woods, not on the Net.

CHAPTER 14

Federal to State Land

The general rule for hunting any public lands, starting with federal lands, is ask first. In the national parks the rules are explicit and sometimes vary from year to year. For instance, usually you can hunt morels in Glacier National Park; however, in 2004 the park was off-limits to mushroom hunters because of the forest fire that devastated the northern part of the park. Likewise, Yellowstone was closed because of the hordes of people who invaded the park after the 1983 fires. (It has since been reopened to mushroom hunters on a limited basis.) In Ohio, Cuyahoga National Park closed its doors to mushroom hunters who came by the busload and damaged the park.

In some national forests, you need a permit, but usually fees only apply to commercial harvesting. Many places have specific regulations and limits. Be sure to ask first. In the northwestern states where commercial mushroom hunting is more common, the rules are more defined. Each year, depending on the burns, the rules vary.

The Corps of Engineers has no specific rules denying mushroom hunting on Corps land. The Corps of Engineers projects are along waterways, which make them especially desirable for mushroom hunting. One close to our home near Kansas City is Smithville Lake, which used to have agriculture, orchards, and forestry. Over the years we have harvested many pounds of morels there for our dinner table. Missouri and Kansas have a lot of lake projects that fall under the Corps of Engineers.

Most Department of Natural Resources (DNR) land, state forests, conservation land, and other public hunting lands are good places to find mushrooms. Remember, morel mushroom season is also turkey season in many states. Be sure to wear safety orange and review chapter 6 for more on safety precautions. Contact the conservation commission in the state you wish to hunt for the wildlife code book and DNR maps, which list numbers of acres for lakes, forestry, and prairie and can be very useful in planning where to hunt. The mushroom hunting information is listed under wild edibles or wild plants in the code book.

You may be required to get a permit. Often these permits are free but you still have to carry one to be legal. All commercial pickers must have a permit. Some states set limits and a few require a state land recreational license.

State parks and state forests have their own regulations by state. Always ask first. To find contact information for your state forester, visit www.stateforesters.org. For instance, in Alaska no person may disturb, damage, deface, or remove trees, plants, moss, rocks, gravel, or minerals unless specifically authorized by the director. A person may gather berries, fruits, mushrooms, and similar edibles for personal consumption but may not sell or distribute them. In Wisconsin the law says that edible fruits, nuts, asparagus, and wild mushrooms may be gathered in state parks for your own use. Except for wild edibles, you may not destroy, molest, deface, or remove any natural growth or natural archeological features. Some states are more mushroom friendly than others.

For county parks, city parks, and nature sanctuaries, check your local phone book to find out who to contact for the rules and regulations. Our area has public use land beside a college campus, and signs are posted in the woods designating the boundaries. In the spring of 2004 a local newspaper printed a story about a woman who hunted on the college land and was stopped by a college security person who confiscated her morels. None of us wants to lose our mushrooms, or worse yet, pay a fine for trespassing, poaching, or stealing. Public land can be great to hunt; just be respectful of the law and other hunters' rights.

WHERE TO HUNT

ALABAMA: OK to hunt public hunting areas (DNR land). State parks, no.
http://www.outdooralabama.com/

ALASKA: OK to hunt all public land, personal use only. OK to hunt in state parks.
http://www.cf.adfg.state.ak.us/

ARIZONA: Most public hunting ground is actually national forest, OK to hunt. State
parks require permission. http://www.azgfd.com/

ARKANSAS: OK on Wildlife Management Land. National forest, OK for personal use
only. State parks, no. http://www.agfc.com/

CALIFORNIA: Department of Fish and Game Land, OK to hunt. State parks, no.
http://www.dfg.ca.gov/

COLORADO: State parks, no. Permission required in national forests.
http://wildlife.state.co.us/

CONNECTICUT: State forests, OK. DNR land, OK. State parks require permission.
http://www.ct.gov/dep/site/default.asp

DELAWARE: State parks, no. Fish and Game Land, no. http://www.dnrec.delaware.gov/

FLORIDA: State parks, no. National forests, OK, personal use only. http://myfwc.com/

GEORGIA: Wildlife Division Land, OK. State parks, no. http://www.dnr.state.ga.us/

HAWAII: Forestry and Wildlife Land, OK, must have permit. State parks, no.
http://hawaii.gov/dlnr/dofaw

IDAHO: State parks, OK. Fish and Game Land, OK. National Forests, OK, personal use
only, 5-gallon limit per day. http://fishandgame.idaho.gov/

ILLINOIS: State parks, OK. DNR Land, OK. http://dnr.state.il.us/

INDIANA: State parks, permission required for each park. National forest, OK.
http://www.in.gov/dnr/

IOWA: State parks, OK. State land, OK. http://www.iowadnr.com/

KANSAS: State parks, OK for personal use only. Department of Wildlife, OK.
http://www.kdwp.state.ks.us/

KENTUCKY: State parks, no, but check with each park for exceptions. State Fish and
Game Land, must have permission. http://www.kdfwr.state.ky.us/

LOUISIANA: State parks, must have permission. Wildlife Management areas, OK, 5-gal-
lon limit per day for personal use. http://www.wlf.louisiana.gov

MAINE: State parks, no. Inland fishing waterways, no. http://www.maine.gov/ifw/

MARYLAND: State parks, no. Wildlife Management areas, OK.
http://www.dnr.state.md.us/sw_index_flash.asp

MASSACHUSETS: State parks, must have permission. Fish and Wildlife land, must have
permission. http://www.mass.gov/dfwele/dfw/

MICHIGAN: State parks, OK, daily use only. State land, OK.
http://www.michigan.gov/dnr/

MINNESOTA: State parks, OK for personal use. DNR Land, OK.
http://www.dnr.state.mn.us/index.html

MISSISSIPPI: State parks, must obtain permission at each park. National Forests,
must have permission. Wildlife Management areas, must have permit.
http://www.mdwfp.com/

MISSOURI: State parks, OK, 2-gallon limit per day. DNR Land, OK.
http://mdc.mo.gov/

MONTANA: State parks, State Land, recreational license required, 5-gallon limit per day. DNRC Land, next door to National Forest Services Land, coordinate rules and regulations as needed. Check specifically when acquiring a license. Particular tracts of land vary. http://dnrc.mt.gov/

NEBRASKA: State parks, no, but check with each park management for exceptions. DNR Land, OK for personal use. http://www.ngpc.state.ne.us/

NEVADA: State parks, OK. DCNR Land requires permission. http://dcnr.nv.gov/

NEW HAMPSHIRE: State parks, no. Wildlife Fish and Game Land, no. http://www.wildlife.state.nh.us/index.htm

NEW JERSEY: State parks, no. State forests, no. DNR Land, must have permission. http://www.state.nj.us/dep/fgw/

NEW MEXICO: State parks and DNR land, no, but check with each park management for exceptions. http://www.wildlife.state.nm.us/

NEW YORK: State parks, OK. State land, OK with permission. http://www.dec.state.ny.us/

NORTH CAROLINA: State parks, must obtain Special Activity Permit. DNR Land, OK with permission. http://www.state.nc.us/environment

NORTH DAKOTA: State parks, no. Wildlife Land, must obtain permission. http://gf.nd.gov/

OHIO: State parks, OK. State forests, OK. http://www.dnr.state.oh.us/wildlife/default.htm

OKLAHOMA: State parks, OK. State forests, OK. http://www.wildlifedepartment.com/

OREGON: State parks, must have permit. National forests, check each for permits and limits. http://www.dfw.state.or.us/

PENNSYLVANIA: State parks, must obtain permission. State Game Land, OK. http://www.pgc.state.pa.us/

RHODE ISLAND: State parks, no, but check for exceptions. Fish and Wildlife land, must have permission. http://www.dem.ri.gov/

SOUTH CAROLINA: State parks, no. May make exceptions, must obtain a clearance letter from state botanist for foraging. National forests, requires permission. http://www.dnr.sc.gov/

SOUTH DAKOTA: State parks, no, but check for exceptions. Game and Fishing Land, no. http://gfp.sd.gov

TENNESSEE: State parks, no. DNR Land, must obtain permission. http://www.state.tn.us/twra/index.html

TEXAS: State parks, no. Wildlife Management areas, OK. http://www.tpwd.state.tx.us/

UTAH: State parks, must obtain permission. National forests, must obtain permission. State Trust Land, OK for personal use only. http://www.wildlife.utah.gov/

VERMONT: State parks and Wildlife areas OK for personal use only. http://www.vtfishandwildlife.com/

VIRGINIA: State parks, no, but check for exceptions. DNR Land, must obtain permission. http://www.dgif.state.va.us/

WASHINGTON: State parks, OK for personal use. Fish and Wildlife land, OK. National forests, check each for rules and limits. http://wdfw.wa.gov/

WEST VIRGINIA: State parks, no. National forestry, must have permission. http://www.wvdnr.gov/

WISCONSIN: State parks, OK. DNR Land, OK. http://www.dnr.wi.gov/

WYOMING: State parks, must have permission. State forests, OK. http://gf.state.wy.us/

Acknowledgments

We would like to thank everyone who helped with this book, including all the folks at the DNR offices, state parks, forestry offices, national parks, Corps of Engineers offices, and national forestry offices. Our special thanks to Cathy and Harry Canterbury of *ASO: Adventure Sports Outdoors* magazine, Tom and Vicki Nauman of Morel Mania, W. W. Bill Willis of the Grand Valley Chapter of the National Wild Turkey Federation, Jason Edge, the Colsons at Jake's Northwest Angle, Kevin Townsend, Bill Foster, Harry Brannen, and all the folks who have shared mushroom hunting with us at sport shows, in the field hunting with us, and online.

We especially want to thank our son, Paul, who mushroom hunted with us every year of his life all across the country, including Alaska. The best part of the mushroom hunt and its prize is the joy of sharing it with family and friends.

Index